Chapter One

Yesterday I walked with a secret. It pressed against my ribs like a stone hidden in a pocket, solid, undeniable, heavier with every step I took. Emma had given me the news, calmly, the way people in her profession must. She was a consultant at the Queens Medical Centre, steady-voiced and unsentimental, but her eyes betrayed her. She had seen this before, seen the pause in someone's chest when the words finally landed, like a glass shattering on tile.

"Cancer," she had said. Not shouted, not whispered—just placed the word between us as if it were a small, fragile object she could no longer carry.

The word did not surprise me. My body had already been speaking, in its quiet, insistent language: the fatigue that settled into my bones like damp, the pain I tried to ignore, the quiet knowing that shadows don't grow without reason. Yet still, when she said it aloud, it was like someone pulling the plug in a bath. The water of me—my certainty, my forward momentum—began to spin away, spiralling anticlockwise down through my legs, into my feet, and then into the floor. I sat there, watching myself drain away.

I left her office with the strange sensation of walking on borrowed legs, as though they belonged to someone else, some sturdier person who could still bear weight. Outside, the world remained stubbornly unchanged. Buses wheezed past, schoolchildren laughed, someone shouted into their phone. And there I was, carrying this new thing, a

Contents

shadow folded into my chest, invisible to all of them.

I walked aimlessly for hours, through streets I barely registered. My mind was not in the present but spiralling back and forth—into memory, into possibility, into fear. I thought of my father, who had died before his time, and wondered if I would follow him into the same dim corridor. I thought of the half-finished projects on my desk, the unread books stacked by my bed, the people I had promised I would visit but never did. How arrogant I had been, assuming there would always be another summer, another holiday, another tomorrow.

By the time I reached the park, the light was low, bruised orange along the horizon. I sat on a bench and watched the ducks gathering at the water's edge. They moved with an

easy rhythm, dipping and surfacing, unbothered by the coming night. I envied them their simplicity.

I tried to imagine telling others, speaking the word aloud myself. Cancer. Even in my head it felt raw, an ember on the tongue. Would people pity me? Would they step back, afraid? Would they tell me to fight, to be strong, as if strength were a currency you could withdraw at will?

I sat until the cold seeped through the wood beneath me and the first stars pricked the sky. Eventually, I rose. My secret rose with me. It would not leave, not yet. It had taken up residence, quiet and patient, waiting for me to speak it into the world.

Chapter Two

The morning after the news, I woke with a decision. Not a loud or dramatic one, but a quiet clarity that arrived with the pale dawn light stretching across my ceiling. If life was now a burning wick, shortening with each breath, then I would not watch it gutter out in silence. I would live—live with urgency, with tenderness, with all the hunger I had once put aside for later. Later was gone. There was only now.

I told no one. The secret remained mine alone, folded like a sealed letter against my chest. To share it would be to fracture the fragile stillness I needed, to invite the noise of pity, advice, fear. I could not bear that. I needed my own silence, my own reckoning.

So I sat at my computer, the blue glow washing across my face, and opened my accounts. Numbers lined up before me, cold and obedient, rows and rows of accumulated years, of careful saving, of waiting. What had I been waiting for? Retirement? A safer season? The promise that there would always be more time? My mortality laughed at the neat columns, at the comfort of totals and balances. Still, I closed debts, moved funds, set things in order. A strange serenity accompanied me, as though each transfer was a ritual, preparing for something greater.

Then, with a keystroke, I leapt. I booked a return flight to Thailand. Not one-way—return. As if to remind myself that there was still a cycle, a possibility of coming back, though the truth was more uncertain. Thailand called to me like a temple bell: meditation, quiet, the slow unwinding of thought in the humid air. A place to sit with mortality, to learn its face without flinching.

When the confirmation email arrived, I stared at the screen, the words pixelated but absolute: Your journey is confirmed. It was not just the journey to Thailand. It was the journey into the last chapter of my life, however long or short it would be.

That evening I walked again, but differently than the day before. The air was sharper, alive with scent and sound. A child's laughter rose like a fountain. A dog barked with

reckless joy. The trees, darkening against the sunset, seemed carved with more detail than I had ever noticed. It was as though life had turned up its brightness, daring me to pay attention.

And I did. Every breath tasted like something rare, like fruit only found once a season. I touched the railing of a bridge and felt the chill of iron, the permanence of matter, and my own impermanence beside it. I whispered a promise into the dusk: I will not waste what remains.

Thailand was not just a place on a map. It was an idea: that healing could exist without cure, that acceptance could grow in silence, that living fully meant bowing to both beauty and brevity. I imagined myself sitting cross-legged in a temple courtyard, incense drifting around me, monks chanting as the sun rose over palm trees. I imagined looking inward, finding not despair but a fierce gratitude.

I had decided. I would live, not just survive. The secret still slept in me, unspoken, but it no longer felt like a weight. It felt like a key.

Chapter Three

Airports have their own silence, even amidst the noise: the silence of people waiting, watching, moving in their separate currents. At Heathrow, as I wheeled my bag through the terminal, I felt the hush of judgment settle upon me. Not spoken, not direct, but implied in the sideways glances, the flick of an eye, the quiet assumptions people make about a man like me boarding a flight to Bangkok.

Thailand has a reputation, and I carried it like a shadow. The brochures speak of temples, beaches, and mango trees heavy with fruit. But the whisper in the background is always the same: cheap living, cheap thrills, and the promise of neon nights where desire is bartered as easily as currency. A single man, middle-aged, travelling alone to Bangkok—how easily the stereotype fit. I could hear the unspoken words: Look at him, another one chasing girls and beer.

Of course, they never said it aloud. But as I sat at the gate, waiting for boarding to be called, I imagined their thoughts wrapping around me like vines. The couple across from me, scrolling through photos of their children, must have wondered why a man of my age travelled alone. The businessman in his suit, tapping at his laptop, probably filed me away under "expat-to-be, chasing a cheap life in Asia." Even the young backpackers, laughing over their rucksacks and Lonely Planet guides, might have glanced my way with suspicion.

I tried to sit straighter, to look deliberate, purposeful. My book remained open on my lap, though I hadn't read a line in ten minutes. It was absurd, really worrying so much about what strangers might think, when they likely never gave me more than a fleeting glance. Yet it mattered. I wanted to tell them: This is not my story. I am not here for indulgence or escape. I am here to meet myself, to reckon with the silence I've carried since the diagnosis.

On the plane, the feeling grew sharper. I watched the passengers around me settle into their long-haul routines— shoes off, blankets tucked, screens flickering with Hollywood films. I imagined each of them creating their private stories about me. A divorced man? A seeker of cheap pleasures? Perhaps even a retiree planning to stretch his pension further in the heat and humidity of Bangkok.

None of them could know the truth—that I had walked with death at my shoulder, that I had booked this flight not out of hunger for excess but out of a hunger for clarity. That Thailand was not an escape but an entrance: into meditation, into quiet, into the slow realisation of what it means to live fully when time is no longer infinite.

I closed my eyes and leaned back, the hum of the engines wrapping around me. For a moment, I let their imagined judgments fade. What did it matter what they thought? My journey was mine alone. Yet part of me still longed to stand up in the aisle and declare it, to change the minds of everyone onboard: You are wrong about me. I am not chasing shadows. I am chasing light.

Instead, I stayed seated, silent. Sometimes silence is the truest declaration. Outside the window, the runway lights blurred into long streaks as we accelerated. Soon, the ground fell away, and London became a scattering of jewels against the night. I pressed my forehead to the glass and whispered a promise only I could hear: Thailand will not define me. I will define what Thailand means to me.

As the plane turned eastward, carrying us toward the unseen dawn, I felt the weight of their imagined judgments loosen. Let them think what they wanted. I was not their story. I was writing my own.

Chapter Four

Bangkok announced itself before I even left the taxi. The sky was still the colour of bruised pearl, a hesitant dawn, but the city was already wide awake. Six o'clock in the morning and the roads were a living organism, a restless body of metal and motion. Small bikes darted between lanes like impatient fish, their engines coughing, whining, then leaping forward. Cars inched and surged, horns sharp as birdsong. My driver navigated Sukhumvit Road with the patience of someone who knew there was no real order here, only rhythm—a rhythm you surrendered to or were consumed by.

The air seeped through the vents, thick and warm, smelling faintly of petrol and something sweeter, like overripe fruit left in the sun. We turned into Soi 11, and the street narrowed to an intimate chaos: food carts already steaming with breakfast, a tangle of power lines scribbled against the sky, neon signs winking even as daylight gathered its courage. I watched it all with a kind of fevered wonder, my body humming with exhaustion but my mind crackling with electricity.

When the taxi finally stopped in front of the hotel, I stepped out and the smell hit me like a shovel—dense, humid, layered with heat and life. It was a smell that belonged to no

single thing but to everything at once: fried garlic from a vendor's wok, wet asphalt still holding the memory of night rain, the faint perfume of jasmine drifting from a nearby doorway. The air wrapped itself around me like a damp cloak. My clothes clung instantly to my skin.

I should have felt only fatigue. My body had been airborne for eleven hours, stretched across time zones, fed on airline meals and recycled air. But sleep was impossible. I was buzzing, as though the city had poured its current directly into my veins. Every sound sharpened—the hiss of woks, the rising chatter of vendors, the sudden high-pitched laugh of a woman on a passing motorbike. Even the light seemed alive, a pale gold spreading across the tops of buildings, promising a heat that would soon become merciless.

The hotel lobby offered a pocket of calm, but I lingered outside for a moment, unwilling to retreat from the sensory assault. I watched a young boy balancing a tray of iced coffees, weaving through the traffic with a grace that defied physics. I watched a monk in saffron robes step lightly across the cracked pavement, his face serene as if the chaos around him were only wind passing through leaves.

This was the Bangkok I had imagined and yet not imagined at all. The clichés of neon nights and cheap pleasures belonged to another hour. Morning Bangkok was something different—raw, unfiltered, unashamed of its own sweat and noise. It was a city that did not apologise for existing in excess.

As I finally entered the hotel, the cool air-conditioning kissed my damp skin, but part of me already missed the street's heat and smell. My room key felt light in my hand, a temporary anchor. I would rest, but only briefly. The city outside pulsed like a drum, and I could not help but move to its beat.

Chapter Five

Night in Bangkok descends like a velvet curtain, thick with heat and promise. By the time I stepped out of the hotel the air had shifted from the bruised warmth of afternoon to something electric—alive with neon and the rhythmic call of nightlife. The street outside pulsed with invitation: music spilling from open doorways, the clatter of ice in glasses, the scent of lime and grilled meat drifting through the humid dark.

In my pocket sat a wad of cash an inch thick, absurd and thrilling. I felt its weight like a dare. Time was no longer a gentle horizon but a cliff edge, and I wanted to lean over it. With only weeks—perhaps months—to live as fully as I could, what use was caution?

The first bar was barely twenty yards from my hotel, a narrow doorway lit by pink and blue lights. I pushed inside and was met with a chorus of smiles. The girls welcomed me with open arms, laughter spilling like champagne as I waved the cash in a clumsy flourish and bought them all a round of drinks. Their voices rose in playful delight, their

bracelets clinking as they clapped my shoulders and tugged me toward the centre of the room.

I felt, for a moment, like a film star—though a foolish one. The lights made everything shimmer: their sequined dresses, the condensation sliding down cold bottles, the gleam of my own sweat. I played the role with reckless joy, letting the music shake loose the weight of diagnosis and dread.

As the night deepened, so did my intoxication. Beer blurred the edges of thought until the world became a kaleidoscope of colour and sound. Two girls decided to join me on my next stop, their laughter like bells as we stumbled into the humid night. Their companionship came at a cost, but I barely noticed; the currency of the evening was pleasure, not prudence.

In the next bar, I met my first kathoey—a Thai transgender woman whose beauty was matched only by her wit. She leaned close to tell me a joke so sharp and unexpected that I burst into helpless laughter, the sound tearing out of me like a release I hadn't known I needed. Her eyes sparkled with mischief as she teased me, and before long she, too, had become part of my growing entourage.

We moved through the city as a small parade: six revellers linked by nothing but music and the urgent need to be alive. Clubs opened their arms to us, bass lines thumping like a second heartbeat. Drinks appeared and disappeared, lights strobed against our faces, and I—the rich farang, the foreigner with pockets of cash—splashed money as if it were water, as if generosity could delay the clock.

Somewhere in the haze I felt the faint tug of awareness—that I was acting the fool, performing excess while mortality waited in the wings. Yet the thought dissolved beneath the music. For one night, I let the city's chaos drown out the quiet certainty of death, and in that roaring dark, I lived as though tomorrow had been erased.

As we reached my Hotel suite the two kathoey and the three girls made themselves comfortable , I sat on the settee with my arms around two women who molested me, music started to play and cloths disappeared, one of the kathoey stripped showing a small penis and started to masturbate right in front of my face as one of the girls sucked my cock, it was an orgy or drink drugs and sex, I knew my flight to Samui was only a few away but this was my one night in Bangkok.

Chapter Six

Morning sunlight sliced through the thin hotel curtains like a blade, illuminating the wreckage of the night. The room was a battlefield of bottles, clothes, and perfume-heavy air, the carpet littered with glittering fragments of memory I would rather not examine too closely. My head throbbed in time with the muffled heartbeat of the city below, a rhythm that mocked my hangover.

Bodies shifted in the haze. Two women stirred on the rumpled bed, their laughter now replaced by the soft rustle of departure. One stretched like a cat, gathering a sequined top from the floor; another hunted silently for a lost shoe. Their movements were efficient, practiced—a quiet choreography of exit. The two kathoey who had lit up the night with their sharp humour and dazzling smiles were already gone.

Gone too, I quickly discovered, were my camera and a small stack of cash. My stomach dropped, a cold plunge against the fevered heat of the room. For a breathless moment I imagined the photos—evidence of my revelry—already finding their way into stranger's hands, a private folly turned public. Then relief crept in: the main stash of money remained safe, hidden before I'd left for the night. I had been reckless, but not entirely stupid.

Still, embarrassment burned hotter than any loss. The images on that camera were not just snapshots; they were proof of a self I barely recognised—this sudden, unrestrained version of me who had danced, laughed, and spent as though death itself had been waiting at the bar. The thought of those photos surfacing, of anyone seeing me as the wild farang splashing cash, tightened around my chest like a fist.

There was no time to dwell. A plane awaited, and the clock showed no mercy. I stumbled into motion: shit, shave, shower, ashore—the old sailor's mantra tumbling through my foggy mind as if it might steady me. I splashed water on my face, wincing at the reflection that stared back: eyes bloodshot, hair dishevelled, skin damp with sweat and regret. Yet beneath the exhaustion, a strange light flickered. I was alive. Very much alive.

As I dressed, the women slipped out with quiet goodbyes, their perfume lingering like a ghost of the night. I watched the door close behind them and felt a curious mixture of relief and nostalgia, as if a dream had ended too soon. My bag waited by the door, packed and ready for the next chapter.

Down in the lobby, the city's morning roar seeped in: tuk-tuks rattling, vendors calling, the endless hum of Bangkok refusing to sleep. I paid the bill, my hands steady now, and stepped out into the already sweltering day. The heat hit me like a reminder—of the chaos I was leaving behind and the fragile urgency that had driven me here.

I had no time to reminisce, no space for shame. The night was gone, the camera gone, the cash mostly intact. What remained was a simple truth: you only live once. And I, foolish and fortunate, was still living.

Chapter Seven

The plane dipped through a curtain of clouds and the island emerged like a promise. Koh Samui glowed beneath the morning sun, a patchwork of emerald jungle and shimmering blue sea. From the small oval window I could see the surf licking the golden shore, the palms bowing in the soft breeze, the distant haze of fishing boats tracing slow arcs on the water. After the dense, neon storm of Bangkok, the sight felt like a cool breath drawn after a fever.

The airport itself was a postcard of calm. Open-air pavilions with wooden beams and slatted roofs welcomed us instead of steel and glass. The air smelled of salt and frangipani. Birds darted between hibiscus flowers while luggage carts hummed lazily across the tarmac. Everything moved at a slower rhythm, as though the island had agreed long ago to refuse urgency.

As I stepped onto the warm ground, the chaos of Sukhumvit and Soi 11 receded into memory. Bangkok still clung faintly to my skin—the scent of smoke, the echo of music—but the sea breeze began to peel it away. My shoulders eased, my breath deepened. It was as if the island itself were whispering: Let it go. You are safe here.

The resort was a gentle miracle. Villas nestled among coconut palms opened onto a beach where the tide whispered rather than crashed. The sand shimmered like crushed pearls, and the sea shifted in lazy shades of turquoise and jade. I felt the night of revelry—the laughter, the beer, the frantic throb of bass—slip from my muscles with every step toward my room.

Once inside, I dropped my bag and stood at the balcony, listening to the slow conversation between waves and wind. My body ached in places I hadn't known could ache: a dull throb in my calves from dancing, a tightness across my shoulders from carrying the weight of both luggage and mortality. I wanted nothing more than to dissolve into the stillness.

I called reception and, in a voice still gravelled by travel and hangover, asked for a massage in my room. "Ten minutes," the receptionist promised, her tone as soft as the breeze outside.

True to her word, a knock came before the clock could mark a full quarter hour. The masseuse entered with quiet grace, carrying a small basket of oils whose fragrance filled the air with notes of lemongrass and warm earth. She spoke little, only a gentle greeting before guiding me to lie down.

The first touch was cool and deliberate, oil spreading like liquid sunlight across my back. Her palms pressed and released, kneading the tension buried deep in muscle and memory. Each movement unthreaded the remnants of

Bangkok's noise: the honking taxis, the clinking glasses, the laughter that had been both joy and escape.

With every stroke I felt myself slipping into a dreamlike place—a soft interior ocean where thought drifted like a boat without oars. Time thinned. The night before ceased to matter. There was only the sound of waves outside and the slow, healing rhythm of hands smoothing away the ache of a body learning, at last, "Would sir like a 'Happy ending?" this did not surprise me as my cock stood erect under the small white towel, she removed the towel and gently started oiling my hard on, "How much?" I asked the girl, she smiled and took off her tee shirt and shorts for me to appraise "1000 Bhat, for full massage "she said with the most mischievous smile, I couldn't refuse the invitation as I nodded my head she straddled me and slowly inserted my cock into herself with great precision and deftness.

Chapter Eight

After the massage—after the slow unravelling of knots and the quiet, unexpected conclusion that left me both relaxed and dazed—I lay still, a thin sheet pulled across my damp skin. The air-conditioning hummed softly, a mechanical lullaby, while outside the balcony door the sea went on breathing. My own breath followed its rhythm, rising and falling in a cadence older than thought.

The world had shrunk to a few sensations: the faint slickness of oil on my shoulders, the gentle ache of muscles finally released, the fading warmth of hands that had guided me somewhere beyond words. Pleasure lingered like a secret, neither shameful nor triumphant, simply a reminder of the body's stubborn aliveness. For a man who had recently heard the ticking of his own mortality, that aliveness felt almost holy.

I thought of Bangkok, of neon nights and clinking glasses, of laughter that masked a desperate hunger. I thought of the two kathoey who had slipped away before dawn, the camera gone, the evidence vanished but not the memory. Each encounter—reckless, joyful, foolish—was already softening into something dreamlike, a collection of moments stitched together by the knowledge that they could never be repeated in exactly the same way.

Lying there, I felt the strange sweetness of impending loss. If death was indeed waiting, I would miss all this: the hum of distant scooters, the salt-stained wind, the simple grace of human touch. Not just the grand gestures, but the small things—the condensation on a glass of water, the way light falls across a stranger's smile, the silent language of hands easing tension from a weary back.

The massage had not cured me, of course. No touch could erase the shadow that followed me from England.

Yet it had reminded me that I was still here, still capable of sensation, of surrender, of joy. The diagnosis had narrowed my future to a pinhole, but in

that narrowness I had discovered a sharpness of life I had never known when time seemed endless.

I closed my eyes and listened to the sea. Each wave was a lesson in impermanence: arriving, breaking, dissolving into foam, and returning again. I imagined myself as one of those waves—temporary, fleeting, beautiful in the brief moment of existence. Perhaps that was all any of us could hope for: to arrive fully, to crest brightly, and to disappear without regret.

The masseuse's soft knock signalled her departure. She bowed slightly, a gesture of quiet respect, before slipping out of the room. I remained where I was, the silence folding around me like warm sand.

A part of me ached to stay on this island forever, to let the sea and the slow rhythm of days wash away the fear of endings. But even as I wished it, I knew that wishing was useless. Life, like the tide, moves forward whether we are ready or not.

For now, I simply lay still, grateful for the body that still breathed, for the heart that still beat, and for the fleeting, aching beauty of a world I would one day have to leave behind.

Chapter Nine

Morning broke soft and pale, the kind of gentle light that makes even departure feel like a blessing. I woke before the alarm, the residue of dreams dissolving into the hush of the room. Outside, the sea moved in a slow, silver rhythm, its surface catching the early sun like a sheet of hammered metal. Today I would leave Samui and cross the narrow channel to Koh Pha Ngan, an island whispered about in traveller's tales—home of the legendary Full Moon Party, and, for me, the meditation retreat where I hoped to quiet the restless tide inside my own mind.

I packed slowly, folding clothes that still carried faint traces of Bangkok's neon and Samui's salt air. The massage oil lingered on my skin, a reminder of the previous night's unexpected tenderness. Each movement felt deliberate, as if the act of placing one shirt atop another might help me fold away the chaos I'd left behind.

The ferry wasn't until midday, which left me with a stretch of unclaimed morning. I wandered down to the beach bar tucked beneath a row of leaning palms. The bartender, barefoot and unhurried, greeted me with the easy warmth of someone who measures time by tides rather than clocks. I ordered a cold beer—the first of a few—and settled onto a bamboo stool with my feet buried in the warm sand.

The sea spread before me in layers of turquoise and jade, the waves lapping softly like a whispered conversation.

Fishing boats bobbed on the horizon, their engines silent as they waited for nightfall. Behind me, the bar played a slow reggae tune, its lazy guitar a perfect soundtrack to the gentle surrender of the morning.

I sipped the beer and felt the quiet seep into me. After the frenetic pulse of Bangkok and the decadent swirl of Samui nights, this small act—a drink in daylight, no agenda, no expectation—felt almost radical. There was no need to chase excitement. The excitement was in the stillness itself: the way the foam clung to the rim of the glass, the way sunlight braided itself through the palm fronds, the way my own breathing began to match the rhythm of the sea.Other travellers came and went—sunburned couples with backpacks, a pair of laughing girls who kicked off their sandals and danced barefoot in the sand—but I remained rooted, content to be an anonymous observer. No one here knew my story. No one needed to. The diagnosis, the nights of indulgence, the unspoken countdown—they all receded like distant waves.

By the time I returned to the hotel, the sky had begun to deepen into a softer blue. I ate a simple dinner of grilled fish and rice, washed down with another quiet beer, and allowed the day's calm to settle over me like a second skin. Sleep came easily, untroubled by regret or anticipation. Tomorrow the ferry would carry me to Koh Pha Ngan, to meditation, to whatever waited beyond the horizon.

For now, the island rocked me gently toward rest, the sea whispering its patient mantra: Be here. Be now.

Chapter Ten

The ferry sat low in the water; a slow-moving beast painted in sun-bleached blues and reds. I stepped aboard with my small bag slung over one shoulder, the wooden planks warm beneath my sandals, and found a place along the open deck. The morning air carried a scent of salt and diesel, a mingling of movement and rest. Koh Samui receded behind us in a haze of palm trees and soft mountains, while the sea stretched ahead like an endless invitation.

The engine's thrum settled into a steady heartbeat as we pulled away from the pier. Foam fanned out behind us, a white seam stitched into the turquoise fabric of the Gulf of Thailand. The boat rocked gently, each rise and fall a slow breathing that coaxed the tension from my shoulders. I leaned against the railing, eyes half-closed, and let the sun lay its warm hand across my back.

Two young women claimed a spot nearby, their laughter carrying easily above the hum of the motor. They looked like the very embodiment of the island's easy freedom: sun-streaked hair, shorts faded from salt water, anklets jangling with each step. One wore a straw hat decorated with tiny shells; the other balanced a guitar case against the bench and immediately began to strum a careless tune.

"Heading to the party?" the guitarist asked, her accent a soft Australian drawl.

I smiled, caught off guard by the sudden inclusion. "Party?"

"The Full Moon," the other chimed in, eyes bright. "Koh Pha Ngan. Tomorrow night. The beach turns into this crazy festival—music, fire dancers, buckets of cocktails. You must come."

I chuckled, shaking my head at the inevitability of youth. "I'm supposed to be going to a meditation retreat," I said, though the words felt heavier than I expected. "Starts in two days."

"Perfect," the guitarist said without missing a beat. "You've got a free night to sin before you start cleansing your soul."

Their laughter was infectious, a lightness I hadn't realised I'd been craving. I imagined myself alone at the retreat, sitting cross-legged while the moon rose over a silent sea, and felt a sudden tug toward the opposite extreme. I had come this far chasing experience, chasing the fragile sweetness of living. Why stop now?

I looked out at the water. The horizon shimmered with heat, a thin silver line where sky and sea blurred into the same endless blue. Two days remained before silence and discipline claimed me. Two days of breathing room, of freedom.

"All right," I said, surprising even myself. "One last blow-out, then I'll meditate my sins away."

The girls whooped in delight, clinking their water bottles against my beer can as if sealing a pact. We spent the rest of the crossing trading stories—of travels, of music, of lives briefly intersecting under the same unrelenting sun.

As Koh Pha Ngan's coastline grew from a faint smudge to a bright green promise, I felt the familiar spark ignite once more. The sea, the sun, the fleeting laughter of strangers: life insisting, again and again, that it be lived before it slips away.

Chapter Eleven

The women had pre-booked two small beach huts, each perched on stilts above a strip of powdery sand. They welcomed me inside with the easy hospitality of travellers who collect strangers like seashells. The huts were simple—bamboo walls, mosquito nets, a hammock strung across the wooden balcony—but the view was priceless: an endless sweep of turquoise sea breathing in slow, hypnotic waves.

While one of them tuned a guitar, soft notes spilling into the warm evening air, I settled into the hammock and let myself sway. The sea breeze stroked my face. The sun, now sliding toward the horizon, painted everything with a gold so soft it felt like forgiveness. The moment held a calm so complete I could almost forget the frantic nights of Bangkok and the uneasy countdown ticking somewhere in my chest.

Amy brought me a drink—something cold, sweet, and laced with rum. Alongside it she placed a tiny square of paper. "Take this," she said with a conspiratorial smile.

I didn't ask questions. I already knew. A tab of something meant to open doors inside the mind. Psychedelia in a postage-stamp. I hesitated only long enough to feel the faint thrill of decision, then placed it on my tongue and washed it down.

The change came gently at first: colours sharpening, music from the beach below rising like smoke, the strum of the guitar floating through the dusk as if each note carried light. The sea's rhythm seemed to breathe inside me. My thoughts loosened, drifting like the tide.

Then a knock rattled the wooden frame of the hut. A man stepped into view—a traveller's cliché come to life: dreadlocks bleached by salt, board shorts hanging low, tattoos crawling across sun-darkened skin. He leaned against the doorframe with a lazy smile, but my eyes snagged on the ink along his neck. For an instant, the tattoo shifted. A devil's head emerged from the tangle of lines, horns curling upward, eyes burning with a red that didn't exist in the real world.

A shiver passed through me. Is he evil? The thought came unbidden, sharp as a blade. I blinked, and the vision dissolved. Just a man again, relaxed and harmless, his tattoo nothing more than abstract swirls of ink. Relief washed over me like a sudden wave.

Before I could steady myself, one of the women arrived and greeted him with a hungry kiss. As their bodies pressed together, the devil returned—his features twisting, a long tongue unfurling as if to devour her. I tore my gaze away, heart pounding, the hammock swaying wildly beneath me.

The trip was too strong, the images too vivid. I rose on unsteady legs and stepped into the night, leaving the laughter and music behind. The jungle welcomed me with shadows and the damp scent of earth. Crickets chirped in hypnotic rhythm. I followed a narrow path beneath palms and vines, each step carrying me deeper into darkness and away from the hallucinated devil, hoping the forest might quiet the storm inside my mind.

Somewhere behind me, the guitar still played, its notes bending and shimmering like light on water—calling me back or maybe urging me to keep going.

Chapter Twelve

By the time I stumbled back toward the shoreline, the jungle path glowing faintly in the moonlight, the edges of the trip had begun to soften. Colours still shimmered with a faint halo, but the world no longer pulsed and bent. The music drew me forward, low at first, then swelling into a rolling thunder of bass and drum.

The beach was alive. Hundreds of travellers moved like a single breathing organism beneath the full moon, their silhouettes flashing in neon paint and flickering firelight. Strings of coloured bulbs draped between palms cast a carnival glow across the sand. Buckets of cocktails glinted under ultraviolet lamps. The sea itself seemed to dance, each wave catching the light as it lapped at the shore.

I paused at the edge of it all, drinking in the spectacle. The air smelled of salt, smoke, and something sharper—sweet and chemical, the perfume of a night built on altered states. Laughter rose and broke like surf. Everywhere I looked, strangers embraced, spun, shouted into the music as if trying to out sing the moon.

Drawn by the hum of voices, I ordered a drink at a beach bar—a plastic cup filled with something luminous and suspiciously blue—and settled onto a wooden stool. From there I could watch the endless procession of faces:

sunburned backpackers, barefoot dancers, couples locked in their own private orbits.

A girl approached, her pupils wide and shimmering. "You holding?" she asked, leaning close so I could hear her above the music.

It took me a second to catch her meaning. "No," I said quickly, shaking my head.

Her shoulders dropped in disappointment. Without another word she spun away, swallowed back into the crowd. I must have looked the part— alone, older, sitting with the stillness of someone who waits for customers. I laughed under my breath at the irony. A man chasing clarity mistaken for a man selling chaos.

The fire dancers took the centre of the beach, their flaming staffs carving bright circles in the night. Sparks arced upward like startled stars. The crowd roared with each daring twist. Beyond them the sea rolled forward, licking the sand with a rhythm older than any party.

Out of the swirl of bodies I spotted Amy. She moved like a slow flame, her hair catching every coloured light as she wove through the crowd. For a heartbeat our eyes almost met—then she vanished into the crush of a beachside bar, swallowed by music and neon.

Something restless stirred inside me. Watching wasn't enough. I wanted to feel the music rather than simply observe it, to let it beat against my ribs until thought dissolved. I drained the last of my drink, its sweetness clinging to my tongue, and scanned the

crowd. Somewhere out there were the sellers, the quiet magicians who turned paper and powder into kaleidoscopes of sound and colour.

The night was still young. My retreat would wait. For now, I stepped off the bar stool and into the thrumming chaos, searching for another doorway into the music.

Chapter Thirteen

I woke with the sunrise, though woke hardly seemed the right word. My mind felt stretched thin, a fragile membrane between dream and daylight. Somehow—by luck, instinct, or some homing call of salt and sand—I had found my way back to the wooden huts. The small balcony, the gentle sway of the hammock, the faint smell of coconut oil

and woodsmoke—they were both strange and familiar, as if the night had rearranged the world while I wandered through it.

The eastern sky glowed like an ember, soft orange bleeding into lavender. As the sun edged higher, it laid a golden hand on the hills that rose abruptly behind the beach, steep green shoulders lifting from the sand. The jungle shimmered with dew, leaves trembling in the newborn light. The sight felt almost holy, as though the island itself was blessing the aftermath of our chaos.

What a night it had been. The memory unfurled in fragments: fire dancers spinning circles of light, music that throbbed like a second heart, strangers whose faces blurred into streaks of neon. I had danced until the line between body and rhythm disappeared, until the question of who I was—or who I was supposed to be—mattered less than the simple fact of being alive.

I lowered myself into the hammock, its ropes creaking softly as it welcomed my weight. The air was warm but gentle, carrying faint threads of last night's music. Somewhere down on the beach, the party still flickered—an echo of bass and laughter dancing on the morning breeze.

Amy had returned while I drifted between sleep and wakefulness. She sat cross-legged on the porch, her hair a tangle of moonlight and sweat, eyes half-closed as she rolled a cigarette. She offered me a quiet smile, the kind that asks nothing and explains even less. In that smile I felt a strange companionship, the unspoken bond of those who have shared a night outside the ordinary.

Laura, though, was still out there. I pictured her weaving through the thinning crowd, barefoot and fearless, her hips moving to rhythms older than language. There was something serpentine in her grace, a charm that could trap without force—like a snake charmer coaxing a cobra from its basket. I wondered if she was still dancing, still luring strangers with that magnetic smile, or if she too had found a quiet corner to greet the dawn.

I closed my eyes and let the hammock rock me. Here, no one asked for a résumé, no one measured worth in titles or years. Here you could shed the skin of who you had been and invent yourself anew. And I had. For one night, I was not a man marked by illness or bound by expectation. I was simply a heartbeat among many, a flicker of joy against the vast dark.

The thought settled like warm sand: I may never get this chance again. Time is a tide, relentless and unknowable. But for now, while the music still floated across the morning air, I had arrived fully in my own fleeting life.

Chapter Fourteen

Amy was the very picture of a seventies dream—a sun-kissed hippy goddess with long blonde hair and a body that seemed sculpted from golden light. She moved with a soft confidence, the kind that came from living unburdened, from knowing the strength of her own beauty. Her bikini clung to her like the memory of salt water, each movement a quiet ripple of grace.

When she stepped inside the hut, the air seemed to grow warmer, heavier with the perfume of coconut oil and ocean breeze. She smiled, a slow, mischievous curve of the lips, and settled beside me on the wide double bed. The world outside—the endless sea, the fading music of the Full Moon party—slipped into a blur. There was only the hush of the room, the pulse of our breathing, the slow magnetism of two bodies finding their way toward each other.

Our laughter rose and fell like a tide, the hammock outside creaking in rhythm as if keeping time. Amy's touch was playful and sure, her hair a silken curtain that smelled faintly of sea salt and smoke. The geckos clung to the bamboo ceiling above us, their tiny eyes glinting like stars, as if they too were curious witnesses to this small miracle of human closeness.

A soft knock broke the spell, and the door swung open to reveal Laura, barefoot and glowing with the afterlight of the party. Her eyes sparkled like the first hint of dawn. She crossed the threshold without hesitation, the energy of the night still dancing in her movements.

What followed was not a collision but a weaving—a slow, wordless merging of laughter and warmth, of arms and hearts. Time loosened its grip. The three of us became a tangle of shared breath and gentle discovery, a quiet celebration of connection in its most human form.

Outside, the tide whispered against the sand. Inside, the world felt infinite—soft light spilling through the shutters, the scent of the sea mingling with the sweet musk of skin and salt. The geckos chirped from their lofty perches, as though cheering us on, tiny guardians of this fleeting paradise.

When at last we lay back against the cool sheets, a stillness settled over the hut. It was not the stillness of exhaustion, but of completion—a silence filled with the knowledge

that, for a brief shimmering moment, we had shared something unbound by time, fear, or the shadow of tomorrow.

Chapter Fifteen

Morning came like a quiet revelation. The light that crept through the bamboo shutters was soft and forgiving, painting the room in shades of pale gold. The sea beyond the hut breathed in slow, steady rhythms, as if the island itself were reminding me to keep breathing too. Amy and Laura still slept, their bodies curved gently beneath the thin sheet, faces slack with the peace that only follows a night spent in pure abandon.

I lay there for a long time, staring at the ceiling where the geckos traced their silent paths. The night before felt almost mythic now—too wild and too tender to belong to the world I had inhabited only a week ago. Back home, life was a careful arrangement of appointments, bills, and quiet dread. Here, in this small hut of salt and shadow, I had been nothing more than a heartbeat among strangers, a body alive and unashamed.

But the tide of reality always finds the shore. The thought of the cancer returned like a slow undertow, tugging at the edges of my mind. It wasn't fear, exactly—fear had burned itself out when Emma first spoke the word. It was more like an awareness, a constant hum beneath every experience. A reminder that time was no longer an endless stretch of road, but a narrowing path whose end was hidden by trees.

Impermanence. That was the word the Buddhists used. Everything passes: nights like this, the warmth of strangers, the very body that carried me through these fleeting pleasures. I felt it keenly now, the truth of it shimmering in the morning light. And instead of despair, I felt a strange, settling peace. If everything must end, then each moment becomes precious, sharpened by its own fragility.

Today I would leave this hut, this temporary paradise, and travel across the island to the Ananda Yoga & Detox Centre. My home for the next couple of weeks. A place of silence and discipline, where the wild intoxication of the Full Moon would give way to meditation, fasting, and the slow work of healing.

The idea of it felt almost absurd after the chaos of the night before. Yet it also felt necessary. I wanted to sit with myself in stillness, to face the truth of my own body without distraction. To see if there was something beyond pleasure and pain—something like acceptance, or even grace.

I rose carefully, not wanting to wake the women. Outside, the sand was cool beneath my feet, the sky a clear and impossible blue. The party was over, leaving only footprints and a few discarded bottles gleaming in the early sun. I breathed in the salt air and let the sound of the sea fill me.

Life was fleeting. But for now, it was still mine. And I intended to meet it fully— whether in the wild music of the night or the quiet breath of meditation. Each step, each heartbeat, each moment: a gift I could still hold, if only for a little while.

Chapter Sixteen

The days at Ananda Yoga & Detox Centre unfolded like soft waves, each one carrying me a little further from the frantic nights of Bangkok and Koh Pha Ngan. The schedule pinned to the welcome board was both comforting and daunting: a carefully balanced rhythm of breath, movement, and stillness. I had come for this, though—a place where

time was measured not by appointments or treatments, but by the rise and fall of the sun.

My mornings began before the heat arrived, when the island air was cool and the sky still carried the faint blue of dawn. At 7:45 I joined the meditation circle, sitting cross-legged on a woven mat while the jungle slowly woke around us. Birds called from the palms, the sea whispered at the edge of hearing, and the teacher's voice guided us inward. At first my thoughts skittered like restless fish—memories of the Full Moon party, the heavy truth of my diagnosis—but gradually the tide of silence pulled me deeper. I began to notice the spaces between breaths, the small pockets of peace that existed even inside a body marked by impermanence.

After meditation came Vinyasa or Yoga Basics, depending on the day. The studio was open to the sea, its polished wood floor dappled with morning light. We moved through sun salutations as the horizon brightened, each pose a dialogue with gravity. My muscles trembled at first, stiff from travel and indulgence, but the practice loosened something inside me. There was no competition here, only the quiet triumph of showing up.

Midday sessions offered variety: Breathwork on Monday, Hatha Flow on Tuesday, Kundalini on Wednesday and Friday. Each class revealed a different map of the body. Breathwork left me lightheaded and strangely euphoric, as if the very cells of my lungs had been rinsed clean. Kundalini brought waves of energy I couldn't explain—warm currents rising up my spine, a tingling reminder that life still moved within me despite the shadow of illness.

By late afternoon, when the tropical sun mellowed to amber, we gathered again for Yin/Restorative Yoga. This was my favourite time: long, surrendering stretches that coaxed both body and mind into release. The scent of frangipani drifted in from the garden. Occasionally a gecko would scurry across the rafters, a tiny companion in our shared stillness.

Some evenings, if the weather allowed, we met on the rooftop for Sunset Aerial Yoga. Suspended in fabric hammocks, we floated above the ground while the sun dissolved into the sea. Hanging upside down, watching the world turn orange and violet, I felt the strange joy of being weightless—if only for a moment, free of everything that bound me to earth.

Day by day, the island's quiet rituals began to stitch themselves into me. The wild, reckless nights of the Full Moon faded into memory, not as shame but as contrast. Here, among the mats and the sound bowls, I felt the steady truth of impermanence. The cancer remained, a silent companion, but it no longer defined every breath.

Life, I realised, wasn't about clinging to any single experience—neither the chaos of neon nights nor the serenity of meditation. It was about living each fleeting moment fully: the rise of the sun, the warmth of a pose, the simple grace of breath moving in and out. For the first time in a long while, that felt like enough.

Chapter Seventeen

Even as the days at Ananda smoothed themselves into a rhythm of breath and salt air, a shadow began to lengthen at the edges of my peace. I would sit cross-legged in morning meditation, eyes closed, listening to the slow inhale and exhale of a hundred lungs, and for a few precious minutes I would float in a soft white light. Then, without warning, the brightness would dim, and a darker hue would seep in like ink through water.

The thought always came the same way: the operation.

Two words that carried a whole universe of fear.

It waited for me beyond the coconut palms and turquoise horizon, beyond the careful serenity of this island. In just fifteen days I would be on a plane bound for the United Kingdom, where doctors in pale blue masks would open the fragile machinery of my body and try to outwit the cells that had betrayed me.

I tried to push it aside. I threw myself into the schedule—early meditation, long vinyasa flows, breathwork that left my head buzzing and my chest light. I drank herbal teas and ate bowls of fruit, letting the sweetness dissolve on my tongue as if sugar alone could hold back the tide. Sometimes, during Yin class, I would surrender so deeply into a pose that I almost believed the cancer was a dream I could stretch away.

But the mind is not so easily fooled. Each time I neared the quiet centre the teachers called Nirvana, the white field of inner light darkened. A faint shadow at first, then a full eclipse. My breath would catch. My heart would thud a reminder: You have to go back. You have to face the music.

At sunset Aerial Yoga, hanging weightless in the orange glow, I caught myself wondering if this suspension was what dying might feel like—a brief, beautiful pause before gravity reclaimed me. The thought didn't frighten me as much as I expected. It simply was.

And yet, beneath the acceptance, a small flame of defiance burned. I wanted more mornings like these. More salt on my skin, more laughter from strangers whose names I might never learn. More time to taste the world before it slipped away.

Fifteen days. The number pulsed behind every breath. I promised myself I would not waste them. Each meditation, each stretch, each mouthful of fresh fruit became a quiet rebellion: proof that life was still happening, still worth savouring, even as the shadow approached.

The operation would come. The outcome was unknowable. But tonight, as the last light bled across the sea and the geckos began their nightly chorus, I sat with the darkness and let it sit with me. We were, after all, travelling the same road—patient and inevitable, like the tide returning to the shore.

Chapter Eighteen

The night boat to Koh Tao waited like a patient creature at the pier, its deck smelling of salt and engine oil. Lanterns swung in the warm breeze, casting soft halos on the dark water. I climbed aboard with a small pack and a heart quickened by the promise of discovery. This journey would be different—no neon haze, no crowded dance floors. Tonight I was chasing a quieter thrill: the chance to breathe beneath the sea.

As the boat pushed away from the island, the engines settled into a deep, steady chug, a heartbeat against the gentle slap of waves. The coastline of Koh Pha Ngan receded into a silhouette of palms and hills, its lights winking like a distant constellation. Overhead, the sky stretched wide and endless. Stars bloomed by the thousands, so bright they seemed to hum. I leaned against the rail and let the night pour over me—warm air, salt spray, the scent of diesel and possibility.

Koh Tao. The Island of Turtles. I had heard divers speak of it in the reverent tones usually reserved for temples: coral gardens, shimmering schools of fish, a world hidden just beneath the surface. Tomorrow I would begin my PADI diving course, a passport to a realm I had only glimpsed on television documentaries and in childhood dreams. The thought sent a delicious shiver through me.

Would I like it? Could I really trust my lungs to a cylinder of compressed air, surrendering to the strange physics of the deep? The question hovered in my chest like a small, nervous bird. Yet alongside the nerves came a surge of anticipation so pure it was almost joy. To enter another world, even temporarily, felt like a kind of miracle— one more chance to live before life narrowed again to hospitals and white rooms.

I thought of the meditation teachers at Ananda, their voices urging us to witness each breath. Soon I would take those teachings underwater, where breath becomes both survival and prayer. Each inhale a reminder of fragility. Each exhale a thread connecting me to the surface. Perhaps that was the lesson all along: to notice, to savour, to keep breathing no matter how strange the landscape.

The boat rocked gently as we crossed the gulf, the black sea gleaming with a scatter of phosphorescence. I closed my eyes and felt the motion in my bones, the steady forward pull toward something both unknown and inevitable. Cancer had taken much from me— certainty, safety, the illusion of endless time—but it had also handed me this night, this star-drenched crossing, this electric anticipation of the world waiting beneath the waves.

I tightened my grip on the railing and let the salt air fill my lungs. Tomorrow I would descend into blue silence and meet the ocean on its own terms. Tonight, I stood under a cathedral of stars, alive with the knowledge that adventure still called, and that for now, I was free to answer.

Chapter Nineteen

Koh Tao greeted me with a quiet that felt almost rehearsed, as if the island knew exactly the kind of restless soul it was welcoming. The ferry eased into the small harbour under a sky so blue it seemed impossible, and the first thing I noticed was the smell—salt and warm earth, with a faint sweetness from the palms. It was calmer here than the other islands, less noise, less urgency. A place designed for breathing.

I found a modest wooden hut just steps from the dive school, a small room with a slatted balcony that looked straight onto the sea. The boards creaked under my feet, releasing the faint scent of old teak as I set down my bag. From my pack I pulled the bright fabric of my newly acquired hammock and strung it between two sturdy posts. Soon I was swaying gently, the hammock rocking in rhythm with the tide, the sea spreading out before me like a polished sheet of silver.

Outside, the island was all tranquillity—waves brushing the sand, longtail boats bobbing lazily in the cove. Inside, I was anything but calm. A churn of thoughts rolled through me, as insistent as the tide. Would I love the experience of diving, or would I panic once the water closed over my head? Could I really trust myself to sink beneath the surface, to rely on a tank of air and a set of hand signals in a world where words are useless?

The instructors called the first step theory, but the word felt too dry for what we were attempting. We spent hours in a shaded classroom, watching videos of divers gliding through coral gardens, learning about pressure, buoyancy, and the delicate etiquette of the underwater world. I listened, took notes, nodded at the right times—but in my chest, the old fear flickered like a pilot light. The idea of descending into silence was both thrilling and terrifying.

A medical check was required before the open water dive, and the casual way it was administered made me chuckle. A quick blood pressure reading, a few standard questions about breathing and past injuries—then a brisk signature that cleared me for entry into an entirely different universe. I thought of the doctors back in the UK, their careful consultations and grim words. Here, on this bright island, a single sheet of paper stood between me and the depths.

As the day stretched toward evening, I returned to the hammock. The sun melted into the horizon, staining the water pink and gold. The breeze carried faint laughter from the dive school, the sound of tanks being stacked and rinsed. Tomorrow I would take my first real dive, cross the invisible boundary between air and sea, life and something other.

The word bucket list drifted through my mind, half amusement, half defiance. People always spoke of ticking off adventures before death, as if life were a ledger to be balanced. But this was more than a box to check. This was a chance to feel the world from the inside out, to surrender to a place where breath itself became sacred.

I swung gently in the hammock, heart quickening with every creak of the ropes. The calm sea reflected the first stars of night, and I wondered if tomorrow I would find the courage to slip beneath its surface—and what truths might rise with me when I returned.

Chapter Twenty

Night settled over Koh Tao with a softness that felt almost deliberate, the sea smoothing itself into a sheet of dark glass as the first stars flickered awake. After a day of theory and nervous anticipation, I craved a little company— and perhaps a small reminder of the world above the water. The Reggae Bar was easy to find. Its wooden frame wrapped snugly around a tall coconut tree, as if the whole place had grown organically from the sand.

Music spilled into the night air: deep bass lines, the lazy strum of guitars, a rhythm that matched the slow heartbeat of the island. Inside, the bar was a patchwork of bamboo stools and mismatched planks hammered into benches. Lanterns swung in the warm breeze, painting the crowd in shifting gold and shadow.

Behind the counter stood an Aussie with sun-bleached hair and the easy grin of someone who had long ago traded schedules for sunsets. "Welcome, mate!" he called, sliding a cold beer across the plank that served as a bar top. I climbed onto a seat and felt it wobble pleasantly under my weight.

The man introduced himself with a name I immediately forgot—he seemed more like an embodiment of the island than a single person anyway. As he poured drinks, a sweet, earthy scent drifted toward me. He held a loosely rolled joint between his fingers, smoking with a casual efficiency that spoke of long practice.

"Homegrown," he said with a wink when he caught me noticing. "Koh Pha Ngan green. Comes over on the same night boat you took. Carried by the mayor himself, or so the story goes."

I laughed, unsure where the truth ended and island mythology began. The Aussie shrugged. "Either way, it's good stuff. Keeps the vibes mellow."

We talked for a long while—about diving conditions, the best dive sites to explore, the quirks of island life. He spoke of Koh Tao with the affection of someone who had arrived for a holiday and simply never left. "Anything you need to know," he said, tapping the bar with a calloused finger, "I'm your man. Gear, good food, even the dodgy stuff. But mostly—just dive, mate. That's why you're here."

The beers went down easy in the warm night, the music a steady pulse that blurred the edges of my lingering anxiety. When he offered the joint, I hesitated only a heartbeat before accepting. The smoke tasted of earth and sea, a slow unwinding of tension that left the stars above me brighter and the hammock of sound around us deeper.

By the time I wobbled back along the sandy path to my hut, the island had settled into a hush broken only by the distant sigh of waves. My head floated somewhere between the reggae beat and the quiet promise of tomorrow's dive. I collapsed onto my thin mattress, the scent of salt and smoke clinging to my clothes, and slipped into a deep, dreamless sleep—grateful for this small night of fellowship before plunging into the unknown world waiting beneath the sea.

Chapter Twenty-One

The morning announced itself with an odd duet: a bird singing some triumphant island anthem and a sudden splat of gecko droppings landing squarely on my forehead. My eyes snapped open to the pale light filtering through the hut's slatted walls. For a moment I lay still, half amused, half disgusted, the salty air thick with the faint whine of mosquitoes. Their night's work was evident on my arms and ankles—small, itchy welts that had me scratching before I even swung my feet to the floor.

Today was the day. My first real dive.

The dive school buzzed with quiet purpose when I arrived. Tanks clanged softly as they were loaded onto the boat, wetsuits hung like patient shadows along the rail. My stomach twisted with a nervous excitement that tasted like both adventure and dread.

Once aboard, the instructor—an affable Frenchman named Marc—ran through the morning's plan. "Mask clearing," he said, smiling as though it were the simplest task in the world. "Easy, but important. You must trust your breath."

I nodded, but trust was not the word I would have chosen.

We descended in stages, following the anchor line into a world that shifted from turquoise to a dusky blue. The first rush of cold water against my face stole a breath, but the regulator delivered its steady hiss of air, reassuring and alien all at once. Bubbles streamed upward in silver torrents, rushing past my ears with a sound like distant applause. It was disorienting—like standing in a wind tunnel beneath the sea.

The exercise was straightforward: let a little water into the mask, then clear it by exhaling through the nose while tilting the frame. In theory, simple. In practice, maddening. The first time I tried, I blew too hard and only forced more water inside. The second attempt left me blinking in a half-flooded blur. Panic fluttered at the edges of my mind—an instinctive, primal urge to tear the mask away and rocket to the surface.

Marc's calm eyes met mine through the wavering light. He signalled again: breathe, try again.

On the third attempt I managed it—a steady exhale, a firm press at the top of the frame, and the water slipped out in a rush of bubbles. Relief flooded me faster than the sea itself. I gave the OK sign, my heart thudding against the wetsuit.

But victory was short-lived. As we descended toward the seabed, the water grew unexpectedly murky, the brilliant coral gardens I'd imagined replaced by a dark, silty haze. Visibility shrank to arm's length. My chest tightened. Instead of gliding through a bright aquarium, I felt as if I were walking into a dream half turned to nightmare.

The pinnacle we were meant to explore jutted upward like the spine of some ancient creature. To steady myself, I reached instinctively for a ledge, fingers brushing against rough marine growth. Marc gestured sharply—no touching. Even here, the smallest grasp could harm life older than my worries.

I hovered awkwardly, legs scissoring to stay balanced, the sound of my own breathing loud and alien in my ears. This was not the easy paradise I'd seen in glossy brochures. Diving, I realised, was less about floating in wonder and more about learning to surrender—to trust the gear, the guide, and the slow, steady rhythm of breath.

As we began our slow ascent, I caught a flicker of colour in the gloom: a lone parrotfish flashing green and purple before vanishing into shadow. For a brief moment, awe pierced the claustrophobia. Maybe tomorrow the water would clear. Maybe the sea was testing me, demanding patience before it revealed its beauty.

Either way, I surfaced with a new respect for the world below—and for the quiet courage it takes to descend into the unknown.

Chapter Twenty-Two

Night slid back across Koh Tao like a velvet curtain, the warm air carrying the faint hum of insects and the deep throb of bass from the Reggae Bar. After a day of masks, regulators, and the strange hush of the underwater world, I felt a pull toward the lively glow of the coconut-tree bar, as if laughter and music could balance the quiet intensity of the sea.

The place was already alive when I arrived. Lanterns swung in the salt-sweet breeze, and Andy, the ever-grinning Aussie behind the counter, lifted a bottle in greeting. That's when I noticed her.

She stood near the edge of the bar, a tall Danish girl with sun-kissed skin and an easy confidence that seemed to radiate warmth. The dive-school logo stretched across her tank top, the faint smell of salt clinging to her like a memory of the ocean. Her laugh carried over the music—low, rich, impossible to ignore. And, yes, she was spectacular in every physical sense: curves like sculpted marble, hair the colour of beach sand after a long day of sun.

I didn't bother to debate with myself. Life had become too short for hesitation. I moved to the stool beside her and nodded to Andy.

"Bottle of beer, mate," I said, then turned with what I hoped was casual charm. "Do you want one?"

She looked at me, eyes sparkling in the lantern light, and smiled—a slow, mischievous smile that made the room tilt just a little. "Sure," she said, her accent soft and melodic. As she reached for the glass, the briefest brush of her shoulder against mine sent a current racing through me.

The night unfolded like a story written by the island itself. Beers flowed cold and easy, joints passed from hand to hand under Andy's watchful grin. He told outrageous tales of island politics—mayors smuggling weed on night ferries, lost divers rescued by dolphins—each story more implausible than the last. We laughed until our sides ached, strangers knitted together by salt, smoke, and the timeless rhythm of reggae.

Somewhere between the third beer and the second joint, the Danish girl leaned closer, her voice soft enough to cut through the music. "Tomorrow we dive again," she said, a playful warning in her eyes. "But tonight is for the land."

That was all the invitation I needed.

Later, back at my hut, the night deepened into a blur of heat and sensation. The thin wooden walls seemed to hum with the island's energy, the sound of waves mixing with laughter and the muffled beats from the bar. Outside, geckos chirped like tiny drummers, urging the night onward. Inside, time dissolved into something primal and wordless.

It wasn't about conquest or even romance. It was about being alive— about surrendering to the raw immediacy of touch and breath, the reminder that I still inhabited a body capable of desire and joy. Somewhere in the back of my mind the shadow of my diagnosis lingered, but it felt miles away, a dark shape beyond the warm glow of the present.

When sleep finally claimed us, the island kept singing: the surf, the music, the soft night air. I knew this evening would stay etched in memory, a bright flare of life against the quiet uncertainty waiting beyond the horizon.

Chapter Twenty-Three

The next morning brought a haze of golden light through the thin curtains of my hut and the faint scent of salt that clung to everything on Koh Tao. Diane—my new dive buddy in every sense of the word—was already awake, stretching lazily on the balcony with a quiet smile that hinted at both mischief and contentment. We shared a breakfast of strong coffee and sweet mango, neither of us mentioning the night before. The silence was companionable, charged with the kind of energy that only a tropical morning can hold.

Our dive boat motored out toward the Chumphon Pinnacles, a series of towering underwater spires rising from the Gulf like the bones of some ancient cathedral. The sea shimmered a flawless cobalt, and the horizon blurred into a single endless line. The air tasted of engine oil and anticipation.

As we descended into the blue, the world above slipped away with surprising speed. The deeper we went, the more the colours shifted—brilliant turquoise fading to dusky teal, then to the deep, almost holy darkness that gathers around the pinnacles. Schools of barracuda wheeled in tight formation, silver streaks moving as one mind, while anemones swayed gently on the rocky towers.

It was there that I met my first triggerfish.

The creature appeared suddenly, like a small, aggressive guardian of some hidden realm. Oval-shaped and thick-bodied, it hovered just above the coral, its bright eyes fixed on me with unmistakable hostility. When I drifted a little closer, the fish darted forward in a sharp, deliberate move—like a tiny dog lunging at a trespasser. My heart gave a startled kick.

Marc, our instructor, had warned us: Stay clear of triggerfish during nesting season. They defend their patch with the dedication of a mother wolf. Diane gestured for me to keep a wide berth, her eyes crinkling with amusement behind the mask. We floated upward in a slow arc, careful not to cut across the invisible cone of the fish's territory. The triggerfish

followed for a few metres, snapping its powerful jaws as if to remind us who owned the reef.

Further down, in the shadowed clefts of the pinnacle, Diane signalled for me to follow her into a narrow passage where the light barely reached. The darkness was alive with movement—shimmering shoals darting like liquid stars. She turned toward me, her silhouette framed by the faint glow from the open water beyond, and suddenly pulled me close.

The sensation was dizzying: the press of her body against mine, the muffled hiss of air through our regulators, the surreal weightlessness of the deep. It was reckless and utterly unforgettable, a stolen moment suspended in a world where sound was nothing but the slow percussion of our own breath. Another unexpected tick on my bucket list, one I hadn't even known I was chasing.

For three days we dove and surfaced, explored hidden coves, and returned to the hammock for long, unhurried afternoons of laughter, smoke, and skin. It was a rhythm of saltwater and desire, each dive a meditation, each night a celebration of the fleeting.

But time, like the tide, never stays still. My return flight—and the surgery waiting beyond it—hovered at the edges of my thoughts. Too much to do, too little time to do it. Koh Tao had given me thrills I hadn't dared imagine, but the horizon was already calling me onward. I knew I had to move, to keep the journey alive before the world tightened again around hospital walls and cold fluorescent lights.

As the boat carried us back toward the island for the final time, I glanced at Diane, her blonde hair damp and glinting in the fading light. We shared a look—no promises, no regrets. Just the unspoken understanding that some connections are meant to blaze briefly and burn bright, like the sun dipping into the Gulf, before disappearing beyond the sea.

Chapter Twenty-Four

Bangkok's Suvarnabhumi Airport pulsed with the organised chaos of departures. The polished floors reflected a thousand hurried feet, the echo of rolling suitcases blending with announcements that rose and fell in a rhythm only seasoned travellers could decode. I stood in the check-in queue with my backpack digging into my shoulders, a thin film of sweat clinging to my neck, feeling both heavy and weightless all at once.

It was a peculiar mix of emotions: sadness for leaving and happiness for having come at all. Thailand had seeped into me like warm rain, filling cracks I hadn't known were there. From the delirious streets of Bangkok to the tranquil shores of Samui, from the neon chaos of the Full Moon party to the silent depths of the Gulf of Thailand, every stop along the way had left an imprint. I had arrived carrying the shadow of cancer like an invisible passenger; now, though the shadow remained, it felt somehow smaller, softened by salt, laughter, and the reckless joy of being alive.

I glanced around the queue. Other travellers wore the same bittersweet expressions—sunburned shoulders, sandy sandals, the faint exhaustion of lives lived hard and fast over too few days. We were all returning to worlds of schedules and obligations, but each of us carried a private stash of memories that no customs officer could confiscate.

Outside, Bangkok still simmered in its eternal heat. The city had tried its best to consume me: the all-night bars, the motorbikes slicing through traffic like blades, the intoxicating collision of smells—grilled fish, incense, diesel, sweat. I had survived it all, even embraced it. Surviving another night in this beast of a city was no small feat.

Now I was heading home, not just to England but to a different chapter altogether. In a week's time, if all went to plan, I'd be stepping out of an airplane door into the open sky at Langer Airfield, beginning a freefall skydiving course. The very thought sent a current of excitement crackling through my tired body. Diving beneath the sea had taught me to trust breath; now I would learn to trust the empty air.

Skydiving. Freefall. The words themselves felt electric. Where the ocean pressed close and whispered in bubbles, the sky would be pure, endless release. To leap from a plane was to surrender completely—gravity, wind, fear—all of it accepted in a single, irreversible decision. I could almost feel the cold rush of air against my face, the earth spinning upward, the paradox of falling and flying at the same time.

As the line inched forward, I caught my reflection in the polished floor: sun-browned skin, eyes a little clearer than when I'd arrived. Beneath the surface, the cancer still waited, a truth I couldn't out-dive or out-fly. But for now, I carried something stronger—a fierce, quiet joy. I had travelled far, lived boldly, and found fragments of peace in places I hadn't dared imagine.

When my turn came at the counter, I handed over my passport with a grin. The journey wasn't over. The next adventure—this time not into the sea, but into the sky—was already calling, and I felt ready to meet it head-on.

Chapter Twenty-Five

Monday loomed like a glowing waypoint on my mental map—the day I would begin my Accelerated Freefall (AFF) skydiving course. After weeks of beaches, islands, and the slow sway of hammocks, the thought of leaping into the open air over Nottinghamshire felt almost unreal. Yet here I was, back in England, bike tuned and ready, planning to ride the twelve miles from my house in Nottingham to Langar Airfield, the heart of British skydiving.

The plan was simple, but the feeling was anything but. As Sunday evening faded into night, I laid out my gear—helmet, gloves, padded cycling shorts—like a soldier preparing for a campaign. My heart thudded in anticipation, a rhythm that no amount of meditation could slow. Thailand had given me temples and oceans; now the English countryside would give me sky and gravity.

The morning of departure broke crisp and pale, the September air cool enough to sharpen the senses. I mounted my bike and began the twelve-mile ride along quiet lanes and hedge rowed roads. Each turn of the pedals was a small meditation on courage. My breath puffed in white clouds while the rising sun burned through a veil of mist. The road stretched ahead like a challenge, leading not just to a drop zone but to an entirely new way of understanding fear.

As I pedalled, the details of the AFF course played over in my mind. Ground school on day one—hours of rehearsing emergency procedures, body positions, and altitude awareness before even setting foot in the aircraft. If the weather held, I could make three or four jumps per day, the instructors said, as long as my performance kept pace with the schedule. Seven levels to complete.

Seven tests of nerve and muscle memory.

I imagined Level 1, leaping from the aircraft at thirteen thousand feet with two instructors gripping my harness, guiding me into the slipstream. I would need to hold the arch of my body like a human parachute, practice locating the ripcord, and—when the altimeter demanded—pull my own chute. The idea of controlling my descent from that height sent a delicious shiver down my spine.

Levels 2 and 3 promised refinement: still two instructors, but a growing independence as I demonstrated better control, enough that by Level 3 they might release me to fly on my own. The thought was both thrilling and terrifying. I pictured the instructors' hands slipping away, the sky stretching out in infinite blue, and me—alone—steadying my body against the rush of air.

Beyond that came Level 4, where only one instructor would accompany me, and I'd begin controlled turns in both directions. By Level 5, those turns would become sharper, faster, a dance in freefall. Level 6 sounded like pure madness: my first solo exit from the aircraft, a back loop to prove I could recover from a tumble, and the introduction of tracking—horizontal flight across the sky. Superman stuff. Finally, Level 7, the full sequence: solo exit, back loop, tracking, turns, and altitude checks, a symphony of skills played out in forty seconds of falling.

As I neared Langar, the broad Nottinghamshire fields opened before me, the flat farmland stitched with hedges and stone farmhouses. Overhead, a single plane droned,

its sound slicing through the morning stillness like a call to arms. My legs pumped harder, fuelled by adrenaline and a flicker of fear.

At the edge of the airfield, a cluster of hangars shimmered in the sunlight. I slowed my bike and coasted to a stop, heart hammering, sweat cooling against my back. This was it: the next step in a journey that had already taken me through jungles, oceans, and the depths of my own mortality.

Cancer still lurked in the background like a silent passenger, but today it had no voice. Today was about wind and altitude, about learning to trust the air itself. I dismounted, wheeling my bike toward the drop zone, and felt the strange, exhilarating certainty that I

was exactly where I needed to be— ready to throw myself into the sky and see what truths awaited me in the long, roaring silence of freefall.

Chapter Twenty-Six

Ground school began with the sharp scent of jet fuel and damp grass rising from the Nottinghamshire airfield. The morning sky was a flat English grey, low clouds rolling in from the west, but inside the training hangar the atmosphere was electric. Posters of skydivers in mid-flight lined the walls, their bodies perfectly curved like living commas in a sentence written across the sky.

The instructor—a compact man with a voice like a bullhorn—wasted no time.

"Arch!" he barked.

Again.

"ARCH!"

Each command struck like a drumbeat, and we obeyed, throwing ourselves belly-down on the padded mats, forcing our bodies into the sacred skydiver posture: hips pressed low, arms and legs extended, back arched like a bow pulled to breaking point. It felt less like yoga and more like an interrogation drill. My spine screamed, my thighs trembled, and sweat pooled beneath my helmet.

"Head back, hips forward! Chin up! Arch, arch, arch!"

I tried to breathe, to imagine the airflow rushing around me at terminal velocity, but all I felt was the ache of muscles stretched beyond reason. This was no holiday. This was the price of flight.

Between repetitions we rehearsed emergency procedures until they burned into muscle memory. Check altitude. Wave off. Pull. If the main chute failed, find the reserve handle. Pull again. Each step had to be automatic, faster than panic. The instructor prowled among us, correcting hand positions, snapping questions like gunfire.

"What altitude do you pull at?"

"Five-five!" we chorused—five thousand five hundred feet.

"And if the main doesn't open?"

"Cut away, pull reserve!"

The words lodged themselves like survival mantras, but deep inside, a darker thought coiled: What if I forget? What if, in the roar of freefall, the ground rushing up like a rising tide, I freeze? What if I miss the altimeter, or doubt the numbers, or simply…don't pull?

As we practised again and again, the question gnawed at me. It wasn't just fear of death; it was the intimate knowledge that my own hand would decide. The parachute wouldn't deploy itself. There would be no instructor tugging the cord for me. At thirteen thousand feet, there would be only sky, air, and the thin thread of willpower standing between life and an empty plunge.

During a brief break, I stretched aching muscles and stared through the hangar doors at the flat green fields of Nottinghamshire. Out there, the earth looked deceptively soft, like a wool blanket spread over the land. In hours I'd be hurtling toward it at 120 miles per hour, trusting fabric and memory to slow my fall.

The instructor clapped his hands for another round.

"Arch!"

We dropped back to the mats, bodies curving like question marks against the floor. My muscles protested, but a flicker of adrenaline cut through the fatigue. This was the torture before the freedom, the crucible before the leap.

Somewhere beneath the pain and doubt, excitement pulsed like a second heartbeat. Soon it would be real—the door of the aircraft sliding open, the wind roaring in, the choice to step forward and claim the sky. And when the moment came, I knew the question wouldn't be what if I don't pull—but rather, how could I ever not?

Chapter Twenty-Seven

The morning air over Langar carried the clean bite of autumn, sharp enough to cut through the jitter of nerves buzzing in my stomach. By the time I climbed aboard the small aircraft with my two instructors, the world on the ground already felt far away—Nottinghamshire's fields shrinking to a patchwork of green and gold as the engine's growl lifted us higher into the pale sky.

Inside the plane, everything narrowed to a single thread of purpose. The instructors checked my harness, tugging at buckles and straps until I felt swaddled in both safety and inevitability. They gave me encouraging nods, but my focus was on the open door ahead, where the sky waited like an endless invitation.

At thirteen thousand feet, the door rolled back. Wind roared in, a wild, living thing that slapped my cheeks and filled my ears with its feral song. My heart thumped like a tribal drum. The instructors gestured, their movements crisp and reassuring: ready, set, go.

And then we were gone.

The first instant was pure chaos—a tumble of sound and pressure, a rush of cold air tearing at my jumpsuit. But almost immediately, freefall revealed its strange paradox. Instead of the stomach-lurching drop I'd feared, there was a sensation of floating. The earth below remained impossibly distant, the sky around me infinite and calm. Wind streamed past at 120 miles per hour, yet I felt weightless, suspended in a silent cathedral of blue.

I arched my body as drilled—hips forward, arms wide, chin up—and the instructors hovered close, their steady eyes locking on mine. I remembered to breathe, to check the altimeter. The numbers spun down in neat, hypnotic increments.

For a few glorious seconds, the view stole everything: the curve of the coast faint in the east, the silver line of the River Trent winding across the fields, the scattered villages like beads on a green quilt. Cancer, hospitals, mortality—all dissolved in the vastness of that sky. I was simply alive, more alive than I had ever been, flying not as a metaphor but as a fact.

Then the ground began its quiet, relentless rise. What had seemed like a still painting now shifted with alarming speed, fields sharpening, roads defining themselves, the quilt becoming earth again. The altimeter ticked toward five-five.

Time to pull.

My hand slid toward the ripcord, fingers brushing the handle with the muscle memory drilled into me through hours of aching arches and shouted commands. Yet a flicker of thought slid into the space between breaths: What if I don't?

What if I simply held still, letting gravity write its own ending?

The idea was both terrifying and strangely serene. A single decision— one refusal—could end everything. The cancer, the fear, the slow decay. Just sky, speed, silence.

But life surged louder. My instructors' eyes locked on mine, urging, commanding. I gripped the handle and pulled.

The chute snapped open with a violent jolt, a sudden upward tug that transformed roaring chaos into quiet.

The world slowed to a graceful drift. Below, the fields stretched in perfect clarity, a patchwork of life waiting to receive me.

As I floated toward the drop zone, steering the canopy with gentle tugs, a laugh broke from my chest—wild, unbidden, unstoppable. I had leapt into the void and chosen, in the end, to live.

Chapter Twenty-Eight

The jump began like any other—calm, methodical, the aircraft door yawning open to the cold blue morning. I'd rehearsed every movement, every drill. After all, I'd already tasted the sky, floated through its vast cathedral of silence. I thought I knew what to expect. But the sky has its own agenda, and that day it decided to teach me humility.

The exit was clean, the arch solid, but somewhere between a minor adjustment of my arms and a flick of my hips, the balance tipped. A single, imperceptible movement set the spin in motion. At first, it felt like a slow pirouette, a lazy turn in mid-air. Then the rotation quickened, the horizon becoming a blurred carousel of blue and green. My body went from a gentle float to a violent corkscrew, spinning flat and fast, the wind clawing at my suit with the sound of a thousand tearing sheets.

The force pressed against me, pinning my arms and legs outward. The sky was no longer a calm companion—it was a centrifuge. My altimeter flashed numbers I could barely read as they spun past in a dizzying whirl. Twelve thousand feet. Eleven. Ten. My mind tried to steady itself, but the earth was everywhere and nowhere at once.

A flash of movement: my instructor, a dark silhouette carving through the air, trying to close the gap. He hovered just outside my flailing reach, eyes wide with urgency. I could see the calculation in his face: get too close and risk a kick, a collision, a second body spiralling into chaos. He stretched his arms in frantic signals I couldn't decipher through the fog of speed and panic.

This is it, a cold, flat thought announced itself in my skull. This is how it ends.

I imagined blacking out, consciousness slipping away as centrifugal force stole the last of my awareness. Somewhere below, the English countryside waited, indifferent. The cancer treatments ahead—the operation, the sterile hospital rooms—seemed impossibly distant, almost absurd. Here was a simpler ending: clean, quick, decisive.

But instinct is older than despair. Deep inside, some stubborn fragment of life refused to surrender. I forced air into my lungs and fought to flatten my body, arching hard against the invisible grip of the spin. My brain screamed for oxygen. My arms trembled with effort. The altimeter blurred—six thousand… five and a half…

At five thousand feet, as if some unseen hand released me, the spin slowed. The horizon steadied. A window of clarity opened. I grabbed the ripcord and yanked with every ounce of strength left in my body.

The parachute erupted with a violent, blessed crack, jerking me upward into sudden stillness. The world snapped into sharp relief—the patchwork of fields, the silver river, the drop zone glinting in the sun. The lines above me were mercifully untwisted, the canopy a perfect dome of life.

I drifted down in stunned silence, my heart pounding with a rhythm older than thought. The instructor landed minutes later, his face a mixture of relief and awe.

As my feet touched grass near the airfield, I felt the paradox settle inside me. I had flirted with death, accepted its cold invitation, and yet—when the choice arrived—I had pulled. I had saved myself.

Perhaps the cancer will still claim me. Perhaps not. But high above Nottingham, spinning in a dance with mortality, I learned something undeniable: the will to live is stronger than any quiet wish to disappear.

Chapter Twenty-Nine

I didn't want to die.

That was the clearest truth to rise from the storm of skydiving, cancer, and chaos.

For all my flirtations with danger—the Bangkok nights, the acid-soaked jungle walks, the flat spin over Nottingham—the will to live burned hotter than any thrill. I wasn't ready to leave behind the mess, the beauty, the books unread.

One week until the surgeon's knife.

Five days.

Five sunsets.

Five dawns.

It doesn't sound like much—until you count it.

Five days is 120 hours.

That's 7,200 minutes.

That's 432,000 seconds.

Enough heartbeats to fill a lifetime if you feel every one.

What could I do with them? No big adventures now. No borderless skies or spinning earth beneath my feet. The next five days would not be about adrenaline. They would be about absorption. Words. Stories. Ideas. The company of minds greater than mine. Reading as an act of defiance: to feed the soul even as the body prepares for battle.

But what to read when time is so cruelly finite? Which voices deserve the final audition before the scalpel and the unknown? I sat with a notebook, ticking down the seconds, and wrote a list—a survival syllabus, a last-minute library of meaning.

Books to Read Before the Knife Falls

Marcus Aurelius – Meditations

For the calm of a Roman emperor who faced mortality with grace. Stoic wisdom to steady the heart.

Viktor E. Frankl – Man's Search for Meaning

A reminder that even in suffering, we can choose our response, and purpose can outlive pain.

Hermann Hesse – Siddhartha

A journey of self-discovery, rivers and silence, the eternal now.

Haruki Murakami – Norwegian Wood

To taste love and loss in quiet, delicate sentences that linger like incense.

George Orwell – 1984

Because truth matters, even in a hospital where machines will measure every beat.

Gabriel García Márquez – Love in the Time of Cholera

Love and mortality braided together in lush, intoxicating prose.

Alan Watts – The Wisdom of Insecurity

For learning to rest inside impermanence rather than flee from it.

Leo Tolstoy – The Death of Ivan Ilyich

A short, searing meditation on the reality of death and the possibility of authentic life.

Rainer Maria Rilke – Letters to a Young Poet

To remind me that solitude is fertile, that the inner life is vast.

Mary Oliver – Devotions (Poems)

Because her poems ask the only question that matters: Tell me, what is it you plan to do with your one wild and precious life?

Five days.

Seven thousand, two hundred minutes.

Four hundred and thirty-two thousand seconds.

Perhaps I won't finish them all. Perhaps I'll only read fragments. But even a fragment of wisdom is a seed. And if the surgeon's scalpel slips, if the cancer claims what skydiving could not, I will leave this world with sentences still echoing in my blood—proof that I lived, that I learned, that I refused to waste the seconds left to me.

Chapter Thirty

Imagine this: a bottle of Château Lafite-Rothschild, resting in the drink's cabinet, the cork never kissed by air, the deep red nectar trapped in glass while the person who bought it slips quietly out of the world.

Imagine the tragedy of never tasting it.

Or a bottle of The Macallan, its amber glow soft beneath the kitchen light. Years of patient aging, a price tag that makes your pulse skip—saved for what? A birthday? A wedding? Some mythical evening when everything finally aligns. But what if that evening never comes?

The thought landed with the weight of a verdict.

I had spent a lifetime waiting. Waiting for "special occasions," for the right dinner party, the perfect guest list, the flawless mood. All the while life itself—raw, unpredictable, finite—was the very occasion I kept overlooking.

That night, surrounded by books and ticking seconds, I uncorked my own small rebellion.

The bottle was my most expensive red—an absurdly priced Bordeaux that I'd once sworn I would never open until the perfect night arrived. The cork slid free with a soft sigh, a whisper of release. The scent hit first: dark cherries, cedar, a faint shadow of smoke. It smelled like everything I had postponed.

I poured a generous glass, the liquid glinting like garnet in the lamplight.

And then I did something reckless, almost sacrilegious. I splashed a measure of that sacred wine into the pan where my steak sizzled, the ruby liquid hissing as it met the hot metal. The aroma lifted in a single, glorious wave—earth, fruit, fire, and defiance.

When I finally sat down to eat, the taste was pure astonishment.

The steak wore the wine like a velvet cloak; the wine tasted even better for having been set free. It was more than a meal. It was a quiet manifesto: use what you love now.

I thought of my wardrobe next. The cashmere jumper folded like a hostage in its drawer, the silk shirt still pinned with a price tag, the Italian jacket hanging like a museum piece. "I'm saving it for best," I'd always said.

For best.

As if the days I'm living now are somehow second-rate, as if the slow drip of ordinary hours doesn't deserve luxury, beauty, joy.

But the countdown to surgery—five days, 7,200 minutes, 432,000 seconds—has a way of stripping life down to its truths. There is no best day waiting around the corner. There is only this day, with its steak and wine and the faint hum of mortality in the background.

So, I dressed for dinner as though invited to my own coronation. The cashmere jumper. The silk shirt. Even the jacket. I sat at my table in full regalia, chewing steak soaked in wine worth more than any restaurant in town, and laughed aloud at the absurd beauty of it all.

If death wants to find me, let it find me wearing my finest clothes, my lips stained with the richest red, living the best right now.

Chapter Thirty-One

God.

The word sat heavy in my mind that night, as if it had been waiting in the shadows all along, patient as a stone. I had used it my whole life without thinking, a reflex more than a belief. Thank God, I'd muttered in a foxhole years ago after a firefight, when bullets snapped past my ears and I somehow walked away unscathed. Oh God, I've groaned in the dark heat of sex, the syllables pulled from somewhere deeper than language. But those moments weren't prayers; they were exclamations, instincts, soundtracks to survival and pleasure. I had never meant them as conversation.

Now, with the countdown to surgery humming beneath my skin, the word began to echo differently.

Should I start now?

Would it matter?

Would some invisible hand meet me halfway if I finally folded my palms and bowed my head?

I stared at the ceiling and tried to imagine Him—capital H—sitting somewhere beyond the clouds. The childhood image floated up first: a bearded patriarch in white robes, half Zeus, half kindly grandfather. That God felt absurd to the adult in me, a character better suited to stained-glass windows and Sunday school stories. Yet the question refused to dissolve.

Was He really there?

I thought of the times I'd whispered Thank God without meaning to. The firefight. The flat spin over Nottingham. The sudden opening of a parachute when death seemed certain. Instinctively, my gratitude had reached for something larger than myself, as though

survival demanded a recipient. Was that proof of something divine, or just the human brain grasping for order in chaos?

Church had never called to me. My parents weren't religious, and the few times I'd stepped inside a sanctuary it felt like theatre—rituals and incense, hymns and robes, the audience mumbling in unison while I remained stubbornly outside the script. Yet I couldn't deny the quiet allure of it now. The idea of walking into a church, breathing in the scent of wood and candlewax, letting the silence gather around me—it sounded almost medicinal. Not salvation, perhaps, but solace.

But would it help?

If I turned to Him now, days before the knife, would that make me a coward or a seeker? Was belief something you could simply decide, like opening an expensive bottle of wine you'd been saving for "best"? Or was faith more like a slow tide, wearing away doubt over years until trust remained?

I remembered a passage from Marcus Aurelius, the stoic emperor whose words had kept me company in these final days: Either there is a God and providence, or there is only atoms and chance. If there is God, all is well. If there is only chance, you can still live nobly. It struck me that the outcome didn't change the task. Live well. Face death with dignity. The rest was speculation.

Maybe God is the name we give to the mystery that keeps us breathing when the parachute opens, or the love that spills from a stranger's smile. Maybe He is the quiet space between heartbeats where fear cannot enter. Maybe He is nothing at all, and it doesn't matter.

I don't know if I will walk into a church before the operation. I don't know if a priest's blessing would soothe the knife's cold edge. But tonight, as I sit alone with the ticking clock of my body, I close my eyes and whisper thank you— to God, to life, to whatever holds this fragile world together.

And for the first time, I mean it.

Chapter Thirty-Two

Time is a trickster.

It stretches itself like warm honey when you're doing something you love, then contracts like a coiled spring when the thing you fear is approaching. The week before surgery felt like a cruel experiment in relativity. Each morning, I woke to a clock that seemed to sprint toward the hospital doors, while the nights I tried to savour slipped through my fingers like smoke.

I thought of Einstein's quip about a minute on a hot stove versus a minute with a beautiful woman. He was right, of course. Anticipation is quicksand. Fear makes the seconds sprint. Pleasure turns them languid, weightless. It wasn't the ticking of the clock that hurt—it was the uneven gravity of emotion.

As I lay on the sofa, the ceiling lamp throwing a slow arc of light across the room, I felt the pressure of those shrinking hours. I had read my books, uncorked my wine, worn my best clothes. But there was still an ache inside me that books and Bordeaux couldn't soften—a human ache, simple and animal.

Loneliness.

My fingers found my phone almost of their own accord. A flick of the screen lit up the room with the cold glow of late-night possibilities. I wasn't looking for love. I wasn't even looking for conversation. What I wanted was something far less complicated and far more immediate: warmth, touch, the quiet reassurance of another body next to mine.

I scrolled through profiles with the detached efficiency of a man shopping for an expensive meal he may never taste again. Faces blurred past—smiles that promised, eyes that teased. I knew what I was looking for. A certain elegance. A softness that carried an edge of mystery. Japanese. There was something about the grace, the precision of beauty, that called to me. Perhaps it was the illusion of control, of refinement, when everything else in my life felt like a storm.

I found her name easily, a familiar face from discreet whispers among men who shared this particular hunger. Her description was simple and unadorned, professional without being cold. An hour of her company for a couple of hundred pounds. Not cheap. Not vulgar. Just... possible.

I typed a message, the words surprisingly formal, as though arranging a business meeting. She replied within minutes—efficient, polite, a faint hint of warmth hidden in the brevity. A time was agreed. An address sent.

When I set the phone down, a strange calm settled over me. The decision was transactional, yes, but also deeply human. In the shadow of mortality, morality seemed suddenly negotiable. What mattered wasn't the price or the pretence; it was the presence. To feel skin against skin, to hear another heartbeat beside my own. To remind myself that I was alive, still capable of desire, still tethered to the physical world even as the clock raced toward the unknown.

Time, for once, felt slower.

The seconds eased their sprint, stretching into a quiet anticipation—not of the surgeon's knife, but of an hour where fear would be silenced by touch, and life, however brief, would be savoured.

Chapter Thirty-Three

Well, that was a waste of money.

When the doorbell rang, a jolt of excitement flickered through the haze of whisky and nerves. She stood there exactly as promised—beautiful, immaculate, a kind of sculpted perfection that almost didn't belong to the same world as my cluttered flat. Her skin was porcelain-smooth, her dark hair pinned with quiet elegance. A scent of jasmine followed her in, delicate and precise. She smiled, polite and professional, and for a moment I felt like a man in control again, the clock momentarily silenced by her presence.

But the body is not so easily fooled.

We went through the motions—soft words, gentle touches—but beneath the surface my mind was already elsewhere. Tomorrow's appointment sat like a lead weight in my chest. The hospital corridors, the surgeon's eyes, the sterile smell of disinfectant—it all crowded into the room until there was no space left for desire. I wanted to be present, to lose myself in her warmth, but every attempt to focus was met by a cold surge of what if.

What if the cancer has spread?

What if this is my last night as the man I know?

What if the scalpel cuts away more than flesh?

She sensed it, of course. Her hands were patient, professional, but no amount of practiced touch could drag me out of that mental undertow. My body refused the script. The anticipation that had seemed so promising hours ago evaporated into awkward silence. I laughed weakly, a brittle sound that hung in the air like broken glass.

She tilted her head, eyes soft with understanding, and asked nothing. There was no judgment, no cruelty. Only the quiet efficiency of someone who has seen this before. I pressed the £200 into her hand, grateful for her kindness even as shame prickled my skin. Half an hour after she'd arrived, she slipped back into the night with the same elegance she had brought in, leaving behind the faint scent of jasmine and an emptiness far larger than the room.

The silence after her departure was deafening. I stood in the doorway for a long time, staring at the dark street, listening to the tick of the hallway clock. Then I turned to the whisky.

The first swallow burned like confession. The second dulled the edges. By the third, the flat began to blur, the tension loosening its grip just enough for the thoughts to creep in again—thoughts of tomorrow, of scalpels and countdowns, of hospital gowns and the possibility of not coming home.

I drank faster, as though I could drown the future one amber gulp at a time. But whisky has a way of sharpening what it promises to soften. With every swallow the appointment loomed closer, the minutes closing in like a tightening noose.

Tonight, even pleasure had failed me.

Tomorrow, the real reckoning would begin.

Chapter Thirty-Four

The night crawled by in fractured pieces, a restless collage of half-dreams and sudden awakenings. One moment I was floating above an endless blue ocean, the next I was back in a hospital corridor that stretched like an Escher staircase, doors multiplying as fast as I tried to open them. Anxiety has a way of bending time—hours that should have passed like water instead stuck to me like wet cloth. By the time a weak morning light finally crept across the curtains, I felt as if I had slept for seconds and aged a year.

I shuffled to the kitchen, body heavy but jittery with nervous electricity. The rituals of breakfast felt absurdly normal: kettle on, sausages in the air fryer, the soft hiss of cooking meat. The smell filled the room with a domestic comfort that clashed cruelly with the thought of scalpels and antiseptic. I sat at the table with my plate of golden sausages and a mug of tea that had already gone lukewarm, trying to pretend it was any other day.

The letter from the NHS lay where I had left it, folded neatly but radiating authority like a sealed verdict. I unfolded it with greasy fingers, the paper stiff and clinical.

ALL PATIENTS SHOULD ARRIVE TWENTY MINUTES BEFORE THEIR APPOINTMENT TIME.

The instruction glared at me in bold capitals, a command rather than a suggestion. Beneath it, the usual details: location of the treatment centre, check-in desk, a polite reminder to eat normally. Eat normally. As if the body understands normal when the mind is screaming. I stabbed at a sausage and forced a bite, each chew tasting of cardboard despite the crisp perfection of the air fryer.

Eat normally.

Arrive twenty minutes early.

It read like the choreography of surrender.

My eyes drifted to the hallway where my bag sat slouched against the wall. Inside were the small things I had decided, after a night of pacing, might matter if I didn't walk back through my own front door: wallet, phone charger, a clean pair of socks, a book to pass the waiting time, the expensive jumper I had finally decided to wear as a shield against hospital chill. A bag containing the sum of my worldly goods, or at least the pieces of them I could carry into the unknown.

Would I walk out of the treatment centre?

The question slithered through my thoughts no matter how I tried to swat it away. Statistically, the odds were in my favour. Rationally, I knew the operation was routine. But fear is not rational. Fear counts every second and whispers every worst possibility until the walls of the room feel closer than they are.

I checked the clock again—still too early to leave, too late to sleep. I chewed another bite of sausage, swallowed hard, and forced myself to breathe. The letter lay open beside my plate, its black letters stark against the white paper.

The instructions were simple. All I had to do was follow them.

Arrive early. Eat normally. Bring only what you can carry.

I looked at the bag, at the jumper folded inside, at the clock inching forward, and wondered if anyone ever truly prepares for the possibility of not coming home.

Chapter Thirty-Five

The changing room smelled faintly of antiseptic and freshly laundered sheets, a mixture that made my stomach churn and settle all at once. I sat on the plastic chair in a paper gown, legs bouncing despite my best attempt to still them. The door opened with a brisk hiss and in walked a petite blonde woman holding a clipboard, her presence immediately brightening the sterile room.

"Good morning, I'm Dr. Lisa Cummings," she said, voice warm but efficient. Her eyes—clear and steady—carried the kind of calm that only comes from years of guiding nervous patients through small storms. She asked a handful of routine questions: weight, medications, allergies. I answered automatically, my mind half-present, half already in the theatre where the scalpel waited.

Then she looked up from her clipboard and tilted her head. "I hear you cycled here?"

I must have told one of her team earlier, though I didn't remember doing it. I nodded, sheepish. Her brows knit into a small, charming frown.

"Please don't cycle home," she said, the concern in her voice unexpectedly personal. "Give yourself a rest today. Promise me."

That single line—don't cycle home—hit like a bell. So I was going home. There would be a ride back. There would be a back to ride to. The weight on my chest loosened enough for me to exhale a breath I hadn't realized I'd been holding since dawn.

Relief washed through me like warm tidewater as I followed her into the operating theatre. The room was bright, almost cheerful, lights bouncing off polished metal and crisp blue drapes. Lisa gestured toward a reclinable bed.

"Shirt off, please, and just relax," she said with a professional smile.

Relax. Easier said than done. Still, I climbed onto the bed and peeled away my shirt, the paper gown rustling like dry leaves. A nurse prepped the area, cool antiseptic biting my skin, and then the local anaesthetic slid under the surface in a series of quick pinches. Numbness bloomed outward like a spreading fog.

As she prepared her instruments, Lisa began to chat, her voice light and conversational. "So I hear you're a diver? Commercial, right?"

I blinked, surprised. "Yeah. Offshore for years."

Her eyes sparkled above her mask. "I'm just a recreational diver myself. Red

Sea, Thailand… nothing like the depths you've seen. Did you ever get down to the Similan Islands?"

And just like that, the sterile room dissolved. We talked about coral reefs and whale sharks, about the nervous thrill of the first descent and the hush of the deep. She asked about the triathlons I'd raced, which led to Scotland, which led to my years in the Royal Marines. Her brother, it turned out, had served too.

The conversation wove around me like a soft net, pulling my mind far from the thought of scalpels and stitches. By the time I realized she had even started, she was already finishing.

"All done," she said with a cheerful finality, tying the last knot in a neat row of sutures.

A nurse dressed the wound and helped me sit up. I half expected a wave of dizziness or pain, but nothing came— only the surreal lightness of sudden freedom. One hour under the knife, a flirtatious exchange with a diver-doctor, and I was walking out whole.

It felt like stepping out of a cage I hadn't noticed until the door swung open. My chest was taped, my heart unbound. I could have skipped down the corridor whistling Always Look on the Bright Side of Life, the Monty Python anthem that had carried me through darker times.

Some things in life are bad; they can really make you mad…

I hummed the tune under my breath as I left the hospital, each step a little brighter than the last. Life—absurd, fragile, ridiculous life—was still mine to whistle through.

Chapter Thirty-Six

Where now? That was the question that stalked me the moment I stepped back into the daylight, the hospital door clicking shut behind me like the end of an old chapter. Yesterday I had been ready to leave this life, to let the final curtain fall with quiet acceptance. But today—the timeline had shifted. The weight I'd carried for months, the one that pressed me toward the exit, had been sliced away along with a small piece of flesh. I was still here. I was alive.

The relief was intoxicating at first, like a drug you don't realize you've been craving. I felt light, unanchored, as if the future had been handed back to me in an envelope marked Second Chance. But the thrill of survival soon gave way to a cold practicality. Life, beautiful and absurd, still required rent. Bills. Food. I could no longer lean on the illusion of an ending to excuse my lack of planning.

The truth was brutal: most of my assets were gone. Savings? Spent. Investments? Liquidated in a haze of last-hurrah indulgence. I'd treated money like sand in an hourglass— something to let slip away before the final grain fell. But the hourglass hadn't emptied. It sat stubbornly upright, daring me to start counting again.

Back in my flat, I sat at the kitchen table with my laptop, the scar on my chest pulling slightly every time I leaned forward. I opened job sites, scrolling through page after page of positions that paid too little or demanded too much. My bank balance stared at me from another tab, a quiet reminder that survival wasn't a poetic idea—it was math.

I fired off applications almost mechanically, tweaking cover letters, lying about my enthusiasm. Warehouse night shifts. Bar work. Delivery driving. Anything that might keep me afloat. Then I saw it: Nottingham Forest FC – Pitch Response Security. Cash in hand.

The phrase cash in hand lit up like a flare in the night. No waiting for payroll, no awkward explanations about gaps in my CV. Quick money, a couple of days' wages to keep the landlord quiet and the fridge humming. I clicked Apply without hesitation.

As I filled out the short form, I imagined it: standing on the edge of the City Ground pitch, floodlights blazing, the roar of the crowd vibrating through my shoes. The job wasn't glamorous—corralling drunk fans, breaking up arguments, watching for idiots who might vault the advertising boards—but there was a kind of poetry in it. I'd be close to the heartbeat of a game I'd loved as a kid, earning cash by simply keeping chaos at bay.

It wasn't a career. It wasn't a grand reinvention. But it was something. A bridge between the death I had nearly embraced and the life that now demanded my attention.

When the confirmation email pinged in, a small spark of excitement lit in my chest. I was back in the game, literally. I shut the laptop and looked around my flat—empty bottles, half-read books, the remnants of a man who thought he was finished. Now all of it seemed to hum with possibility.

Where now? Forward, I supposed. One shift, one day, one rent payment at a time. Yesterday I had planned my exit. Today, I was planning my next paycheck. Life, in all its cruel, comic timing, had called my bluff.

Chapter Thirty-Seven

The stitches pulled every time I moved, a faint tug beneath the bandage that reminded me I was not quite whole. Standing at the edge of the pitch, high-vis vest catching the glare of the floodlights, I could feel each heartbeat vibrate against the fresh wound. My chest itched beneath the fabric but I dared not scratch. The crowd swelled around me, a living, breathing mass of noise and movement. Sunderland fans—thousands of them—packed into their section like a restless tide.

I told myself I didn't want trouble. I didn't want to test the seams that held me together, either literal or metaphorical. My job was simple: keep my eyes open, stand my ground, respond if things got out of hand. But football is a game of sudden turns, and fans are creatures of passion. When Sunderland scored, the away end exploded in a roar that seemed to shake the very foundations of the City Ground. The noise was physical, a wall of sound that hit me in the chest harder than any punch could.

I saw them then—a cluster of men surging forward, faces red with triumph and beer. The barrier shuddered as they leaned into it, a wave threatening to spill onto the grass. Training took over before thought could intervene. I sprinted, the scar tugging like a warning with every stride.

One of the lads made it past the first line, a wild grin plastered across his face. I stepped in front of him, arms wide. "Back, mate," I barked, but he wasn't listening. His eyes were fixed on the pitch, on glory, on chaos. The swing came out of nowhere—a quick, mean jab to the gut.

Pain bloomed like a firework, white and sharp, but I held my ground. My stitches held too, mercifully. Two of my teammates closed in, grabbing the lad by the arms and dragging him back into the crowd. The rest of the surge faltered, momentum lost. Behind me, play resumed as if nothing had happened.

The adrenaline lingered long after the final whistle. My stomach ached where the punch had landed, but the wound beneath the bandage remained intact. No blood. No tearing. Just a dull reminder that I was alive and still capable of taking a hit.

Back in the staff room, the supervisor handed me a plain white envelope—my pay for the evening. Cash. Heavy with possibility. I tucked it into my jacket pocket like a secret. Outside, the night air smelled of fried onions and damp concrete.

I walked home along the dark streets of Nottingham, the noise of the match still humming in my ears. My legs ached, my chest throbbed, but there was a quiet satisfaction in the weight of that envelope. It wasn't a fortune—just enough for a few pints and a hot meal—but it was earned. Not the reckless spending of a man preparing to die, but the modest reward of someone who, against all odds, was still living.

As I turned the corner to my flat, I wondered what else might lie ahead. Beer tonight, maybe a steak if I was feeling extravagant. Beyond that? I didn't know. The future was a blank page again, and for the first time in a long while, I was curious to see what I might write on it.

Chapter Thirty-Eight

The stitches itched like mad. Each movement reminded me of their presence, the thin black threads tugging against my skin as if they were holding back not just flesh, but the restlessness beneath it. I'd counted the days, followed every instruction: keep it clean, don't strain, avoid heavy lifting. But now the healing was done, the wound sealed, and still the damn things remained—like tiny, stubborn reminders of vulnerability.

I started with the hospital. "Hi," I said to the receptionist, flashing my most reasonable smile. "I had a small operation here last week. Doctor said the stitches could come out today. Can I get an appointment?"

The woman barely looked up from her screen. "We don't remove stitches," she said, as if announcing the weather. "Your GP will do that."

"Right," I replied, swallowing irritation. "Thanks."

Next stop, my GP's surgery. A different receptionist, same flat tone. "You'll need to book a nurse appointment for suture removal," she said. "Earliest we have is next Thursday."

Next Thursday? The word throbbed in my head. My chest felt like a knitting project gone wrong.

"What about the Emergency Centre?" I asked, already dialling as I left the surgery.

"Not our service," the voice on the phone told me. "We don't remove stitches. Best see your GP."

Around and around I went, the loop tightening like the threads in my skin. Each dead end made the itch worse, more maddening. By the time I got home I was pacing, tugging at my shirt, imagining the knot of black nylon buried in the scar.

How hard could it be? The thought arrived quietly, almost reasonable. I'd watched enough survival shows. I'd been a Marine. I'd stitched and unstitched kit, patched wetsuits and cut fishing lines. Skin wasn't that different, was it?

I set up in the bathroom, the light buzzing overhead. A pair of nail scissors, a pair of tweezers, a splash of antiseptic. I laid everything on a clean towel, like a surgeon preparing for theatre. The mirror reflected a man I barely recognised—half-grinning, half-scowling, eyes bright with a strange excitement.

I peeled back the dressing. The scar looked neat, almost smug, a faint pink line stitched like a crooked railway track. My fingers hovered over the first knot. Snip, pull, done.

But then a memory flashed—Doctor Lisa's voice in the operating room, calm and steady, distracting me with stories of diving and triathlons. I imagined her frown if she could see me now, bathroom surgery on a Tuesday evening, Monty Python's whistle still echoing in my mind.

I hesitated. Infection. Scarring. The small but undeniable chance of making a mess.

The scissors clinked softly as I set them back on the towel. I exhaled, half-laughing at my own recklessness. Maybe I'd give it one more day. Maybe I'd keep pestering the GP until they caved.

For now, the stitches remained—tiny black reminders of survival, stubborn proof that life, like healing, refuses to be rushed.

Chapter Thirty-Nine

"Never live your dream."

The words circled my head like gulls over an empty pier. They weren't mine originally; I'd read them somewhere years ago, a throwaway quote in a magazine or a forum post. But now they had become a truth I felt in my bones.

For months, my life had been about escape — not living, but escaping. Thailand's chaos and beaches, diving on Koh Tao, the full-moon neon madness, the women, the skydiving, the wine, the whisky, the expensive food I'd saved for "best." Every tick on the bucket list had felt like oxygen at the time. But here I was, sitting in my flat again, a white scar across my chest, an empty bank account, and that quiet sense of anticlimax.

I'd lived my dream — and now, I was still alive.

The question that lingered was brutal: what now?

If the first half of this book has been about escape — running from death, running from the weight of diagnosis — then maybe the end must be about returning. Not to what I was before, but to something else entirely. Something built.

It struck me, sitting there with the last of my pay from the football match, that my story so far had been one of consumption. Travel, sex, adrenaline, wine. All experiences meant to fill me up. But maybe, just maybe, the second half of life — however long that might be — had to be about creation.

Creation of what, though?

The scar across my chest tingled as I thought about it. Maybe writing. Maybe helping. Maybe working at that diving school in Thailand and teaching newbies how to clear their masks. Maybe becoming an instructor at the dropzone, showing people how to arch, how to breathe, how to face the sky without fear.

For the first time in months, I wasn't thinking about what to spend, or what to drink, or who to sleep with. I was thinking about what to give. What to build.

"Never live your dream," the saying goes, because once you do, you'll be left with nothing. But maybe that's wrong. Maybe once you've lived your dream, you finally have the courage to build another one — not a fantasy to tick off, but a life you can stay inside.

I pictured myself back in Thailand, but not as a tourist or a dying man running from time. As someone who wakes before sunrise to help others meditate at the retreat. Or standing at the edge of the airfield at Langer, the smell of jet fuel in the air, coaching first-timers on their AFF jumps.

I didn't know which of those futures would be mine. But I knew this: for the first time, my story wasn't about dying anymore. It was about living. Living with intent. Living as someone who has been to the edge and come back.

And maybe that's where the book ends — not with a bang, but with a turning. Not a bucket list ticked off, but a door quietly opening to a new room. A place where you stop being the man who is "almost gone" and start being the man who is here.

Alive. Scarred. Broke. But here.

Chapter Forty – Living Forward

The morning came soft and pale, not with the rush of anxiety I had grown used to, but with a kind of stillness. I lay in bed listening to the faint hum of the city — buses groaning to life, bins being rattled down pavements, the muted shuffle of a world that carried on regardless of scars, surgeries, or the weight of dreams fulfilled. For the first time in months, I wasn't thinking about what I had lost. I was thinking about what I might build.

The scar across my chest had stopped itching. It sat there quietly, a line of evidence, a reminder that I had been cut open and stitched back together, and yet still here I was. It didn't feel like weakness anymore. It felt like a badge, a map of where I had been.

I made coffee, strong and black, and sat at the kitchen table with my laptop. The flat around me was littered with remnants of the old life: empty bottles, books bought in a rush to fill the void, the expensive jumper draped carelessly over a chair, worn only once. These were the relics of a man who thought he was dying.

But the man who sat at the table now was different. Not healed, not entirely whole, but turning toward something.

The email draft had been sitting open since last night. Subject line: Re: Possible Position at Ananda. I read over the words again, steadying myself.

"Dear Ananda,

I stayed with you this year. It changed me.

I'd like to return, not as a guest, but to work. I can teach diving, fitness, skydiving theory, meditation — whatever helps.

I want to give back."

It wasn't polished. It wasn't grand. But it was honest.

My finger hovered over Send. For a moment, doubt whispered: Was I good enough? Would they even want me? What if it was just another dream, another indulgence dressed up as purpose? I thought about it, let the questions rise, then let them pass. Doubt had been steering me for too long.

I clicked Send.

It felt like a parachute opening. Like surfacing after holding my breath too long underwater. A small action, yet monumental. The ripple of possibility expanded outward from that single click.

I leaned back in my chair, sipping coffee, and thought about everything that had brought me here: the madness of Bangkok, the full-moon chaos, the laughter of strangers, the feel of salt water against my mask, the fear of spinning out of control in the sky, the relief of pulling the cord and knowing instinct had saved me. Even the failures — the nights I drank too much, the encounters that left me hollow, the mistakes that cost money and pride — all of it had been part of the crash course. A crash course in being alive.

Now came the test: could I do something with it? Could I give rather than only consume?

Outside, Nottingham stirred. A kid's laughter floated up from the street. A dog barked. Somewhere down the road, a man whistled a tune I recognised instantly — Monty Python's Always Look on the Bright Side of Life. I laughed out loud, the timing absurd, perfect.

Maybe I didn't need to know exactly where this new road would lead. Thailand, diving, teaching, volunteering — it didn't matter yet. What mattered was that I had stopped running from death and started walking toward life.

I closed the laptop, stood up, and went to the window. The day looked ordinary. Grey clouds, damp pavements, people rushing to work. But to me, it looked like a beginning.

"I don't know how long I have left," I said aloud, as if testing the words against the air. Then I smiled. "But from now on, I'm living forward."

Epilogue – The Scar and the Horizon

The scar is still there. It will always be there. Some days it itches, other days I hardly notice it, but most days I run a finger across it and remember. It isn't a mark of weakness anymore. It's proof. Proof that I came close to the edge, proof that I wanted to let go, proof that I chose — however reluctantly at first — to stay.

The road ahead is not mapped out. Maybe I'll return to Thailand, maybe I'll take a job guarding football pitches or teaching people to dive into the unknown. Maybe I'll fail again, fall again, spin out again. But that's living.

What I know for certain is this: I no longer measure my life by how close I am to death. I measure it by how much of myself I give, by how deeply I breathe, by how many mornings I wake up and whisper, I'm still here.

I once thought I had lived my dream and there was nothing left. Now I see the truth: dreams don't end. They change shape, they shift, they grow new wings.

So I'll walk into tomorrow — scarred, broke, uncertain — but alive. And that is enough. For today, and for as many days as I'm given.

Printed in Dunstable, United Kingdom